LAURA MORELLI'S AUTHENTIC ARTS

FLOREE

A Travel Guide To Frames, Jewelry, Leather Goods, Maiolica, Paper, Silk, Fabrics, Woodcrafts & More

Published in the United States of America.

LAURA MORELLI'S 🗡 AUTHENTIC ARTS

Library of Congress Control Number 2015931969

Paperback ISBN: 978-1-942467-02-1

eBook ISBNs: 978-1-942467-00-7 (epub), 978-1-942467-01-4 (mobi)

Graphic Design: Shannon Bodie, Bookwise Design

Laura Morelli's Authentic Arts: Florence /Authentic Arts Publishing. —1st ed.

Image Credits:

COVER: © danielito via Morguefile. **EPIGRAPH:** © fcarucci via depositphotos. **INTRODUCTION:** © ifeelstock via depositphotos. **CHAPTER 1:** p. 2 © CPhilip via istockphoto; p. 5 © via depositphotos; p. 7 Michelangelo Buonarotti, *David*, Galleria dell'Academia, Florence © Steve Hanna CC via Flickr; p. 10 © Laura Morelli courtesy of Patricia Morelli; p. 13 © Antonio Gravante via fotolia; p. 18 Luca della Robbia, *Bust of a Young Girl*, Bargello Museum, Florence © Russell McNeil CC via Flickr. **CHAPTER 2:** p. 20 © Lorenzo Patoia via istockphoto; p. 24 Castorina © KotomiCreations CC via Flickr; p. 26 © Giorgio Magini via istockphoto; p. 27 © intagliofirenze CC via Flickr; p. 31 © Lorenzo Patoia via istockphoto. **CHAPTER 3:** p. 34 Agnolo Bronzino, *Portrait of Bia de Medici*, Uffizi Gallery, Florence, CC via Wikimedia Commons; p. 39 © Artigianato e Palazzo, CC via Flickr; p. 40 Benvenuto Cellini, *Salt Cellar*, Kunsthistorisches Museum, Vienna, CC via Wikimedia Commons; p. 42 © Artigianato e Palazzo, CC via Flickr; p. 45 © ksiamal via depositphotos; p. 46 © gumbao via depositphotos. **CHAPTER 4:** p. 48 © danielito via Morguefile; p. 52 © Romuald Le Peru, CC via Flickr; p. 55 © Artigianato e Palazzo, CC via Flickr; p. 56 © Steven Allan via istockphoto; p. 60 © Antonio Gravante via fotolia. **CHAPTER 5:** p. 62 © Museo della Ceramica di Montelupo Fiorentino via eosarte.eu; p. 65 Apothecary jar (possibly the workshop of Giunta di Tugio) © Metropolitan Museum of Art, New York 1975.1.1061, courtesy Open Access for Scholarly Content (OASC); p. 69 © Madonna and Child, workshop of Andrea della Robbia © Metropolitan Museum of Art, New York 49.7.62, courtesy Open Access for Scholarly Content (OASC); p. 71 © Artigianato e Palazzo, CC via Flickr; p. 77 © Laura Morelli. **CHAPTER 6:** p. 80 © Malgorzata_Kistryn via depositphotos; p. 84 © Artigianato e Palazzo, CC via Flickr; p. 87 © siberianwarcat via istockphoto. **CHAPTER 7:** p. 90 © monsieur paradis CC via Flickr; p. 92 wool © Lorenzo Tomada CC via Flickr; p. 96 © AvalancheZ via istockphoto; p. 98 © tupungato via depositphotos. **RESOURCES:** p. 102 © stocknshares via istockphoto; p. 115 © Jon Gonzalo Torrontegui CC via Flickr; p. 120 © clarita via Morguefile; p. 123 © Giuseppe Moscato CC via Flickr. **AUTHOR PHOTO:** Sarah DeShaw

CONTENTS

FREE DOWNLOAD

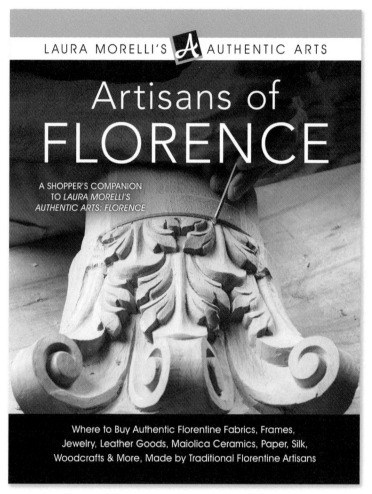

LAURA MORELLI'S AUTHENTIC ARTS

Artisans of
FLORENCE

A SHOPPER'S COMPANION
TO *LAURA MORELLI'S*
AUTHENTIC ARTS: FLORENCE

Where to Buy Authentic Florentine Fabrics, Frames,
Jewelry, Leather Goods, Maiolica Ceramics, Paper, Silk,
Woodcrafts & More, Made by Traditional Florentine Artisans

Join my mailing list and get a free copy of the
companion book, *Artisans of Florence.*

Visit www.LauraMorelli.com/Florence-ReaderGift
to get started.

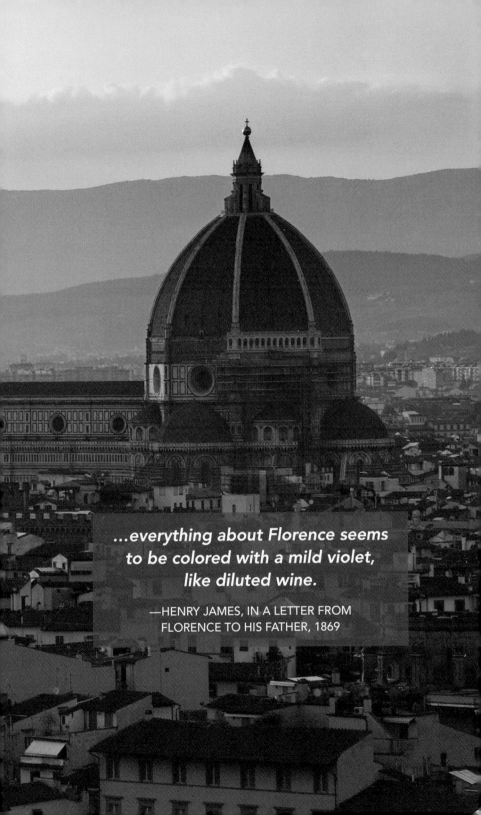

...*everything about Florence seems to be colored with a mild violet, like diluted wine.*

—HENRY JAMES, IN A LETTER FROM FLORENCE TO HIS FATHER, 1869

f you hold even a passing interest in art history, it's hard not to fall in love with Florence. In this birthplace of the Italian Renaissance, beauty, order, and a classical aesthetic breathe life into every street, every square, every building, and every bridge. Florence's native sons—Botticelli, Brunelleschi, da Vinci, Donatello, Giotto, Michelangelo, and many others—still inform the way that the Western world views painting, sculpture, and architecture. Their legacy makes Florentine culture a timeless benchmark of beauty and technical excellence.

As I pursued my own studies in art history, I couldn't wait to travel to Florence to witness those famous masterpieces firsthand. When I arrived, however, I discovered that *living* artists were practicing centuries-old Florentine traditions in workshops and studios across the city. I found masters of leather etching gilded scrolls into belts and bags; women weaving silk on three-century-old looms; fifth-generation bookbinders punching letters into the spines of ancient texts; goldsmiths using their great-grandparents' tools; even a master carrying on a three-hundred-year-old tradition of making powdered wigs. I realized that these unsung heroes quietly carried on a legacy unbroken from the time of medieval guilds. I couldn't believe that while so many visitors knew about Michelangelo and da Vinci, so few knew about these *living traditions* and their makers.

It became my mission to lead travelers beyond the tourist traps, helping them discover authentic traditions and their makers, and come home with great treasures in their suitcases. My focus is cultural immersion through a greater appreciation of artistic traditions and the people who still practice them. It's impossible not to want to take a little piece of Florence home with you. In our world of mass production, many of us yearn for unique, culturally authentic, and immersive experiences. I can think of no better way to appreciate Florentine culture than by experiencing the stories, the people, and the beautiful objects behind the timeless traditions of this captivating city of art.

How to Shop in Florence

Take one glance at the hundreds of leather jackets flapping in the breeze in the San Lorenzo market, and you will realize how overwhelming shopping in Florence can be. We all want to come home from Florence with a special souvenir, but selecting which leather bag or gold bracelet is the right choice can be intimidating. How do you know if you're buying something authentic and high quality, something made locally and in a traditional way? How do you gauge how much you should pay, and how do you know if you're being ripped off? How do you determine if you have fallen prey to one of the city's many tourist traps? High-pressure sales tactics, the plethora of brand-name knockoffs sold on the street, and a dizzying array of high- and low-quality merchandise marketed alongside one another in the same shops and markets, make for a confusing shopping experience.

Is the pursuit of authenticity worth all the trouble? You bet. Learning about the authenticity of Florentine craft traditions immerses you in the history of the city and the spirit of the Florentines themselves. In fact, I would argue that it's one of the *best* ways to experience Florence from the inside out, ensuring that you'll go home with memories—and hopefully a meaningful souvenir—to treasure for a lifetime.

The craft traditions of Florence are deeply embedded in the city's history, arguably more so than in any city in the world. From the twelfth century onward, the Florentine craft guilds, the *Corporazioni di Arti e Mestieri*, dominated the city's economic and social organization. The seven major guilds (*arti maggiori*), five middle guilds (*arti mediane*) and nine minor guilds (*arti minori*) organized the lives of all craftspeople, from painters to sculptors, furriers to cobblers, and makers of everything from hats to belts, keys, bracelets, goblets, rugs, lamps, spoons, shoes, and stockings. Each maker had a role to play in Florentine society, and each contributed to the city's culture of high technical skill, reputation for quality, and economic might.

By the late Middle Ages, every neighborhood of Florence pulsed with the lifeblood of these trades. The ruling Medici family only served to bolster this already thriving culture of artisanal expertise by patronizing makers of fine objects in silver, gold, stone, textiles, and other materials. This intense flourishing of artisanal production helped pave the way for Florence to take its rightful place as the artistic capital of the Renaissance. Today, this spirit of excellence and technical skill continues to pervade Florence, giving the city its particular flavor that draws art lovers from around the world.

A fifteenth-century map known as the Carta della Catena, now conserved in the Friedrich Museum in Berlin, Germany, depicts the massive city walls and segmented quarters of Florence at the dawn of the Renaissance. Historically, artisans were scattered across the city, with small concentrations of tradespeople involved in the same or related trades. For example, at the end of the fifteenth century, tanneries were located along the Arno, while goldsmiths clustered in the Santo Spirito neighborhood before moving to the Ponte Vecchio and surrounding streets a century later. Many other artisans occupied the poorer sections of the Oltrarno district on the southern bank of the Arno River.

NAVIGATING FLORENCE

Every city in Italy has its own confusing address system, and Florence is no exception. Florentines commonly refer to each neighborhood by the main church that anchors it. For example, central Florence is divided into Duomo, San Lorenzo, San Marco, Santa Croce, and Santa Maria Novella. The only exception to this rule is the Oltrarno or the "across-the-Arno" quarter.

Throughout the city, Florentine businesses are marked with an "r" after their street number for *rosso* (red). Residences are marked with an "n" for *nero* (black). Unless you realize this at the outset, finding your destination can amount to a fool's errand, as the numbers quickly run out of sync!

Today, many makers of traditional wares still cluster in the Oltrarno, especially around the Piazza Pitti and the via Borgo San Frediano. I love this section of town, since it preserves the character of an Old World artists' neighborhood, similar to the Left Bank of Paris. It's full of *caffès*, hole-in-the-wall restaurants, and combined studio / living spaces.

Some Florentine artisans break the tradition of closing at lunch in order to accommodate tourist traffic during the busy seasons. Most stores and businesses, however, follow the Italian tradition of opening around 9:00 or 10:00am, then closing around noon or 12:30pm for the midday meal. A two- or three-hour siesta can be frustrating for some international travelers who are unaccustomed to the midday hiatus and are trying to pack as much as possible into the day. There is not much to do about it other than sit at a table and order a glass of Chianti and a plate of pasta, so enjoy! Most shops reopen around 3:30pm, and remain open until around 7:30 or 8:00pm.

Keep in mind that many of the individual workshops you will want to visit and buy from may not adhere to this schedule at all. As many are sole proprietorships or small family businesses, it is not uncommon to find an artisan studio inexplicably closed. Sometimes you will find a note on the door indicating what time they expect to return; other times you may find the shop battened down during regular business hours with no indication of their plans to reopen. It's all part of the serendipity of immersing yourself in Italian culture, so keep an open mind.

In the following sections, you will find specific guidance on how to recognize quality and value in the most traditional Florentine arts. If you follow these guidelines, when you do find a treasure, you will know it beyond a doubt, and the cheap souvenirs and knockoffs lining the streets will fade into the background. The richness and tradition of Florentine authentic arts make sorting through the tourist traps to discover a treasure not only worth the effort, but especially rewarding.

The Spirit of Florentine Arts

A fiercely independent spirit—a strong sense of "us" and "them"—characterizes the people of central Italy, and this is especially true for the Florentines. That passionate independence accounts for centuries-old battles between Florence and its rival, Siena. It accounts for how mere hilltop villages like Montelupo Fiorentino became ceramics meccas, exporting their colorful wares all the way to Constantinople and beyond; and it's how it came to pass that a particular type of embroidery is known even today as the "Assisi stitch." Tuscans are ferociously proud of their culture and their native arts.

Of the central Italian city-states, Florence grew to predominate the region, politically, economically, and artistically. By the 1400s, artisans of all stripes worked diligently to supply the needs and whims of nobles and newly rich merchants in Florence. A lucrative international silk and wool trade filled the coffers of Florentine traders and inspired artisans to create luxurious designs for clothing, church vestments, and other rich textiles. Nobles commissioned ceramic artists to create "his-and-hers" plates ornamented with the elegant profiles of bride and groom to decorate the newlyweds' homes. Just outside of Florence, ceramicists in the towns of Montelupo Fiorentino and Sesto Fiorentino created commemorative vases with coats of arms to mark important political alliances between families. The wives of Florentine bankers shopped for gold earrings and bracelets on the Ponte Vecchio.

Henry James's description of Florence as "colored a mild violet, like diluted wine" sums up the beautifully muted yet rich tones of the city. Florentine style is deeply rooted in the Renaissance, and the city's colors seem to have leapt from the palette of a Renaissance painter—from the warm ochre of the cathedral's terra-cotta roof, to the soft, crackled yellow stucco walls of centuries-old palaces, to the weathered brown wood of hulking arched doorways that lead into buildings and from one section of town to another.

In the history of Western art, Florence plays a critical role. Prior to about 1300, stonemasons, goldsmiths, painters, and other "makers" were organized into a strictly regulated guild system. The master, following a set of guild statutes, ensured that apprentices and journeymen worked their way up the ranks over many years of practice and well-defined stages of accomplishment, thereby passing established traditions on to the next generation. Customers regarded these "makers" collectively rather than individually, even though their works—from gold jewelry to silver goblets—were highly valued for their beauty and symbolism of social status. The patron who commissioned and paid for the work—whether it was a fine chair, a stone sculpture, a gold necklace, or even an entire building—was more likely to get credit for it than those who designed or constructed it.

All of that changed around 1400, when, for the first time, people began to regard painters, sculptors, and architects in a different class from, let's say, a goldsmith or a hat maker. In Florence, a new cultural ideal that would later be called "Renaissance humanism" was beginning to take form. Florentine intellectuals began to spread the idea of reformulating works of classical Greece and Rome, and to place greater value on individual creativity than on collective production. A divide appeared between those who valued such novelty and those who sought to maintain tradition. A few brave Florentine painters—who for many centuries had been paid by the square foot—successfully petitioned their patrons to pay them on the basis of individual artistic merit instead.

In the course of a generation, the work of some Florentine painters, sculptors, and architects rose from the status of "artifact" to "art." And while the makers of traditional objects such as candlestick holders, ceramic vessels, gold jewelry, or wrought-iron gates continued to be seen as faithful laborers who would be recognized communally in trade guilds, a few of their counterparts—virtually all of them painters, sculptors, or architects—rose to international and lasting fame as the rock stars of the Renaissance.

Paradoxically, the new concept of "art" did little to stem the demand for those old-fashioned ceramic vessels, gold jewelry, or wrought-iron gates. In fact, Florence continued to boast one of the strongest guild systems in all of Europe, and its *arti* continued to flourish well into subsequent centuries. In fact, the ruling Medici family counted itself among history's greatest supporters of the so-called "minor arts." The Florentine family made it a cultural policy to offer legal protections for goldsmiths, leather workers, and other craftspeople, and at the same time the family directly commissioned works for its extensive private collection. The competition that resulted from Florentine craftspeople to win the favor of the ruling family resulted in some of the most beautiful and technically masterful objects in the history of art. Even a brief visit to see the Medici private collection in the Pitti Palace's Silver

Museum will give you an appreciation for the jaw-dropping beauty and sumptuousness of which Florentine craftspeople were capable.

After the decline of the Florentine Republic near the end of the sixteenth century, the distinctive Florentine spirit continued to pervade the city's artistic traditions. Today in Florence, many of the trades of the past remain living traditions. The medieval guilds may be long gone, but their arts, their techniques, and their soul still thrive in Florence. The skills, the forms, the knowledge, and more importantly, the spirit of the past, is kept alive in the hands of a small number of individuals who take pride in their city's unique visual essence.

What to Ask Before You Buy

In Florence, it's not easy to choose an authentic souvenir. This is true now more than ever before, as increasing numbers of low-quality leather goods and knockoffs flood into Florence, imported from overseas and passed off as authentic. Recently art organizations have worked to develop trademarks and new alliances to help protect their artistic heritage and to guard against

fakes and cheap imitations. Legal regulations have also tightened; however, there is no substitute for a knowledgeable buyer. If you know what you are buying, you can put your money where it counts: back into the pockets of Florentine makers and not into those of importers looking to make a quick profit without any connection to Florence at all.

Over years of searching for individuals following authentic, centuries-old artistic traditions, I have developed five questions to help guide you through the minefield of shopping in an unfamiliar environment. If you can come up with a good answer to each of the following questions before you purchase your Florentine souvenir, chances are you have picked a winner.

1. Is it traditional and locally made?

Before you travel to Florence, read up on its handcrafted traditions. If you're reading this guide then you're already well on your way! What sparks your interest? Gold jewelry? Stationery? You may have a leather jacket or bag in mind, but have you considered a wallet or change purse? Go online or to the library and read up before you go. Even a cursory education will help you avoid impulsive and reckless purchases that you may regret later.

As soon as you arrive in Florence, train your eye at the museums that display collections of authentic traditions such as silver, gilded wood, and other handcrafted works with a long history. Florence boasts an unusually large number of wonderful and little-visited collections of authentic arts. After spending even a short time in these specialized collections, you will begin to absorb Florentine colors, patterns, styles, and forms. Most of all, you'll be better equipped to spot high-quality, traditionally made wares when you begin to hunt for a souvenir. You can find a list of great museum collections of Florentine arts in the Resources section at the back of this book.

MADE TO MEASURE

One of the most wonderful things about Florence is that you can find a craftsperson to make just about anything your heart desires. From custom shoes and suits to stationery, books, clothing, and furniture, a Florentine master can turn your dream into reality, creating a truly one-of-a-kind treasure just for you. It may not be as expensive as you might expect. Just ask!

In Florence, stick to Florentine-made objects. It's not a good idea to buy Italian goods made elsewhere, such as Venetian glass or Sicilian coral jewelry; purchased out of their local context you cannot even be sure they were made in Italy.

There are two good reasons for buying Florentine works in Florence. First, you are more likely to get a better deal by buying from the source. Second—and even more valuable—is that you are more likely to make a connection with the person who made your purchase, and that will become part of an immersive travel experience that you will carry with you forever.

2. Who made it?

Buy directly from the maker whenever possible. It's your best guarantee that you will go home with a high-quality, handmade item at the best possible price. The added bonus of getting to know the maker of a handmade wooden frame, for example—and perhaps even watch it being made—is invaluable.

Where can you find these makers? In Florence, it's easier than you may think to find them if you know where to look. Throughout this guide, you will find recommendations for specific neighborhoods and streets where you will find working artists clustered together—near the Pitti Palace, in the Oltrarno district's alleys, near the Borgo San Frediano, and scattered on the streets north of the Ponte Vecchio, for example. Makers of authentic ceramics lie outside the city in Montelupo Fiorentino and Sesto Fiorentino. Once you decide what you want to buy, refer to the following chapters and the Resources section at the back of the book for specific recommendations.

3. Who is selling it?

It's always best to buy a souvenir directly from its maker, but if for some reason that is not possible or practical, here are a few other options. One choice is to buy at one of the annual events and festivals that take place in the city. Check the Resources section for specific events where you can find artists who may not maintain a studio open to the public but meet buyers face to face at

GREAT AUTHENTIC
WINDOW-SHOPPING IN FLORENCE

If you want to skip the chain stores and international fashion brands to get a more intense flavor for the authentic arts of Florence, explore these streets:

- **Artisan workshops:** via Borgo San Frediano, streets surrounding the Piazza Pitti

- **Antiques** (but see What Not to Buy in Florence, below): via Maggio, via Santo Spirito, Borgo Ognissanti, Borgo San Jacopo, via de Fossi

- **Art and furniture restorers:** Piazza Pitti, side streets off the Borgo San Jacopo

- **Gold jewelry:** Ponte Vecchio and streets to the north

Now, where should you not buy? As a general rule, avoid the tourist-oriented retailers that lie along major pedestrian thoroughfares of the city, particularly the Ponte Vecchio (see Chapter 3 for more specific guidance about the famous bridge and further recommendations for buying gold jewelry in Florence). Avoid buying from street stalls or trinket shops surrounding the major tourist sites of the city, such as the Uffizi Gallery, the Galleria dell'Accademia, the Duomo, the Piazza della Signoria, the train station, and similarly crowded venues. In these areas you are nearly guaranteed to overpay for a lower-quality item that may or may not have been made in Florence.

these events instead. Another option is to buy from one of the city's museum stores. Museums typically maintain a high quality standard when it comes to items sold in their shops, with a focus on local tradition. However, these options rank far behind the opportunity to observe and interact with local artists. Florence is a year-round extravaganza of richness and culture. Why not avail yourself of the opportunity?

When it comes to buying direct, get as specific as possible. In other words, instead of buying a leather wallet that catches your eye in a boutique window, head to a leather-making workshop and buy directly from the person who made it. You've already come this far; go see how it's made and meet some leatherworkers face to face!

4. How much should I pay?

How much to pay depends on many individual factors. Antique furniture and maiolica ceramics tend to command some of the highest prices of all the Florentine traditions, along with goods purchased in the flagship stores of famous Florentine designers like Gucci and Ferragamo. Some custom gold jewelry can also prove pricey because of the great number of hours and creativity that must go into crafting each piece. On the other end of the spectrum, some of the greatest values can be found in the category of portable leather accessories like change purses and wallets, as well as handmade paper and books. The following chapters outline specific guidelines that will show you what to look for and how much you should expect to pay.

When buying handmade, traditional wares, price and quality do not always correlate. In other words, a high price does not necessarily mean high quality, and a low price does not necessarily mean that the item is less valuable. Value depends on what you buy and from whom, and this is especially true in a city like Florence, where the same item may be sold in venues from a high-end boutique to a street stall. The high-traffic tourist streets command high prices for everything, no matter the quality. Pay attention to your surroundings; if most of the shops on the street cater to international tourists, your risk of overpaying for a lower-quality item is high. Instead, head to the quieter, less frequented quarters of town like the side streets of the Oltrarno, known for their authentic makers.

Remember: a truly authentic souvenir does not have to be expensive, but it may end up being the most *valuable* thing you bring home from your trip to Florence.

5. How will I get it home?

This question is important to ask before separating yourself from your money. There are two aspects of transporting your souvenir that you need to consider.

First, decide whether you will carry the item with you or ship it home. Portable souvenirs like a handbag or a gold necklace are ideal for carrying or wearing on the plane. You may be tempted to transport fragile items like ceramics in your carry-on luggage, but remember that if something breaks, you will not have much recourse to replace it once you've boarded the plane.

Bulky or fragile items, or souvenirs such as knives or letter openers that may not pass airport security, can be shipped. I do not recommend using the Italian (or any country's) postal system, for the simple reason that—even if you've insured it—you will not be able to walk down to the post office and file a claim if your package never arrives. Stick with one of the major international carriers such as FedEx or UPS so that you can insure and track your package. Check your carrier's web site ahead of time to get an idea of shipping rates and times. Some merchants are set up to take care of shipping for you, and may even have special packing materials and containers that are ideally suited to protect fragile items. Don't forget to exchange contact information with the merchant and don't leave the shop without your tracking number.

The second thing to consider is clearing Customs when you arrive home. The Customs services of most countries post specific regulations on their web sites to guide you through importing goods purchased overseas. Most Americans who travel abroad are familiar with the U.S. restrictions on certain food items like fresh cheeses, wine, and chocolate, but did you know that there are additional regulations related to art objects and items that might fall into the category of "cultural artifacts"? It's a good idea to check your country's Customs web site for a list of items that may be restricted or tariffed before you make a purchase in Florence or anywhere else overseas.

AM I BEING RIPPED OFF?

Florence is one of the top destinations in Europe and is generally safe for travelers. Like any popular city, however, it has its share of scams aimed at tourists. Problems range from pickpocketing and purse snatching (sometimes from moped-riding thieves), to illegal "brand-name" handbags sold on the street, to overpriced Florentine-looking souvenirs that were actually made elsewhere. If you want to make absolutely certain to avoid being scammed, ask yourself before buying: Is the item traditional to Florence? Do I know who made it? Am I buying it directly from the person who made it? If you answered yes to these three questions, then chances are you do not need to worry about becoming the victim of a scam, and you can rest assured that you're paying a fair price for the item by Florentine economic standards.

WHAT NOT TO BUY IN FLORENCE

Antiques: If you are an antiques fan, you'll find it hard to resist the beautiful antique shops on the southern bank of the Arno. Keep in mind, though, that prices are extremely steep. You can find better deals at markets and smaller towns in the countryside outside of Florence. However, with all the wonderful discoveries in Florence, you are likely to find something you simply can't live without, so if your budget allows, Florence is a great place to splurge!

Ceramics: You will pay top prices for maiolica wares in Florence as prices are marked up for the lucrative Florentine tourist trade. Nearly all the ceramics you see in Florence are produced in Montelupo Fiorentino or Sesto Fiorentino, both just on the outskirts of Florence (see Chapter 5). It's worth it to make a half-day or day trip if you intend to buy ceramics.

Ready to Buy?

When you are finally prepared to hand over your cash or credit card, go through this checklist:

- ✓ Is the item traditionally Florentine and made locally?
- ✓ Do I know who made it?
- ✓ Am I buying directly from the maker or from a reputable source?
- ✓ Am I getting good value for my purchase (not only in monetary terms but also in terms of an immersive travel experience)?
- ✓ Is the item portable, or worth so much that I am willing to incur the cost and risk of shipping it home?

If you can answer "yes" to these five questions, then you probably picked an authentic Florentine souvenir you will treasure for a lifetime. *Complimenti!*

Frames, Gilding,
& Other Woodcrafts

f I had to recommend a single traditional art to bring home from Florence, it would be one of the ornate, gilded wood-crafts that fill the workshops of the Oltrarno's narrow alleys. Considering their quality and uniqueness, lamps, frames, and other small wooden or gilded items are typically a great value for the price.

Historically, the guild known as the *Arte dei Legnaiuoli*, bearing the symbol of an ax on its coat of arms, regulated Florentine carpenters' professional activities. Their sawdust-filled workshops dotted the right bank of the Arno, clustered along the via Tornabuoni, the via dei Servi, and near the churches of Santa Trinita and Santa Maria Novella. Florentine carpenters specialized in certain types of production. Some focused their work on making domestic furniture like chairs, dowry chests, tables, and beds, while others concentrated on interior decora-tion such as wall paneling and cabinetry for finer homes. Still others plied their trade by making wine barrels, crates, and trunks. For church patrons, specialty woodworkers turned out gilded picture frames, triptych forms that would be finished by painters, huge wooden doors, and vast numbers of church furnishings from lecterns to wooden statues, liturgical objects, reliquary boxes, and other works. For the city of Florence, they constructed the gigantic, iron-studded doors that pierced the city walls.

During the Middle Ages and the Renaissance, Florentine carpenters sourced most of their wood from the Tuscan countryside, relying heavily on walnut, cypress, chestnut, pine, and elm, and selected specimens based on the project and the desired qualities of the wood itself. In its guild statutes, the *Arte dei Legnaiuoli* specified which types of wood were required for different types of furniture. Guild inspectors ensured quality control and adherence to the rulebooks by dropping into workshops to inspect details from the dimensions of a chair, to the construction techniques and joinery of a cabinet, to the types of wood used.

ELABORATE COLLABORATIONS

Historically, Florentine carpenters were required to work well with others, because their craft was fundamentally collaborative in nature. They built and prepared wooden panels to be handed off to altarpiece painters. They created wooden frames that would form the backbone for stone inlay and veneers. Their work was passed on to upholsterers to finish pieces of furniture; metalsmiths to attach hinges, locks, and metal adornments; and other specialized craftspeople to put the finishing touches on a multimedia work of art.

Rarely, however, was wood left in its natural state. Florentine master woodworkers developed complex and refined techniques that included inlaying precious metals and intricate marquetry. They lavished gold leaf on everything from altarpieces to jewelry and frames. It is this elaboration of wood that forms one of the distinctive qualities of Florentine woodwork.

Wood-turning was used to craft table and chair legs, bedposts, and other decorative pieces. Relief carving became a common technique for embellishing furniture and interior decorative elements. *Pastiglia*, which involved covering the wooden surface with linen, then successive layers of gesso, became important in the fifteenth and sixteenth centuries, and allowed for intricate patterns to be crafted. Today, this technique is still popular among Florentine makers of frames.

Marquetry, the art of layering different types and colors of wood across the surface of a piece, became one of the most popular woodworking techniques in Florence. *Intarsia*, a technique closely related to marquetry, became one of the city's most distinctive art forms. Sometimes referred to as *commesso* or *pietre dure* in Florence, this mosaic-like technique involved gouging out a pattern in the wood, and then filling in the pattern with semiprecious materials (onyx, ivory, and other stones). Some of the intricate designs created with this technique—including cityscapes, landscapes, and other scenes—are truly breathtaking, resembling paintings in stone.

Florence is one of the few cities in the world where you can still readily watch traditional woodworkers and restorers at work. Beautiful furniture and wooden embellishments not only played an important role in Florentine artisanal history but remain a vibrant part of the city. Even when it incorporates more modern woodworking tools and technology, the simple, understated beauty of Florentine furniture and woodcrafting has stood the test of time.

Traditional Types of Florentine Woodcrafts

Church Decoration

Some of the most elaborate of Florentine woodwork was destined for churches across the city. Specialized woodworkers crafted paneling, altars, and choir stalls that made up part of a church's permanent interior decoration. Church patrons also commissioned countless reliquaries, candelabra, tabernacles, and freestanding statuary of saints, angels, and crucifixes. Though many of these pieces began with wood, most were elaborated further with painting, gilding, and the incorporation of gems and precious metals.

Domestic Interior Design and Furniture

In contrast to the sumptuous woodwork reserved for church interiors, most furniture designed for use in Florentine homes—even wealthy ones—remained relatively heavy and plain. Medieval and Renaissance furniture in Florence was understated, with block-like forms and restrained decoration, both painted and carved. Chairs, tables, beds, and other utilitarian furniture were massive, imposing, rectilinear, and dignified. Florentine carpenters used basic woodworking tools like the saw, adz, and chisel to craft benches, chairs, chests, and tables. By the fifteenth century, dovetail joinery had replaced the medieval mortise-and-tenon technique of assembling this sturdy furniture.

For the most part, Florentine homes were dark spaces, with small windows to help mitigate the summer heat. They relied on a few important pieces of furniture for storing linens and other household implements. Residents pushed these large, chunky chests, benches, cupboards, armchairs, and side tables against the wall, leaving a sparse open space in the center of the room.

In spite of their simplicity, many household furnishings were prized family possessions passed from generation to generation. One of the most important pieces of domestic furniture was the *cassone*, or dowry chest. At first glance, the *cassone* seems simple enough: a rectangular box with a lid. These marriage chests, however, were costly and highly valued from the late Middle Ages through the Renaissance period in central Italy. These chests contained the bride's trousseau, and were therefore precious and made to last a lifetime. Some of the world's great museums hold examples of Florentine dowry chests of simple and remarkable beauty.

Though most Florentine homes during the medieval and Renaissance periods remained modest, wealthier merchants, bankers, and patrician families of the city demanded more elaborate decoration of their domestic interiors. For these wealthier patrons, carpenters used rarer materials for cabinetry and interior paneling, such as olive wood or ebony. For the richest

THE DOORS OF FLORENCE

Some of the most impressive examples of Florentine woodwork are reserved for doorways, so keep your eyes open for these breathtaking works of art. Most visitors will be led to Lorenzo Ghiberti's famous bronze doors of the Cathedral Baptistery. However, even some of Florence's most modest wooden doors leading to homes or businesses might be elaborately carved, then ornamented with beautifully crafted hinges, locks, doorknobs, doorknockers, and studs of bronze or iron. Every church in the city boasts beautiful doors that usually incorporate masterful works of wood and metal. In my opinion, though, some of the most amazing doors in Florence are those that once secured the city walls, and led from one quarter of the city to another. The wooden doors of the old Porta Romana and the Porta San Frediano, for example, stand some ten times the height of a grown man, and incorporate carved wooden panels, giant metal bolts, and impregnable-looking locks.

Florentine families—the Medici, the Rucellai, the Strozzi, and others—the revival of classical antiquity influenced their taste in architecture and interior design, so woodworkers followed these conventions. Decorative relief-carved motifs such as swags, birds, shells, fruit, and plants appeared on the walls. Florentine master carpenters carved decorate patterns in low relief across the surface of their walls, with intricate paneling, including wooden fluted pilasters with capitals of the classical orders. Many of these more elaborate works involved not only carpenters but also the work of blacksmiths, painters, gilders, and masters of intarsia.

Frames

Throughout the Middle Ages, central Italian artists painted on wooden panels, not canvas. Thirteenth-century documents describe the construction and preparation of these wooden panels with linen and gesso. Many elaborate panel paintings were

religious scenes destined for ecclesiastical patrons, but sometimes, individual patrons also commissioned multimedia works for private chapels or domestic spaces.

Carpenters played a key role in preparing the wooden armatures of panel paintings, as the wooden forms were not considered separate like a frame would later be, but rather an integral part of the paintings themselves. Woodworkers of the 1200s and 1300s constructed elaborate architectural shapes for multi-paneled paintings called diptychs, triptychs, and polyptychs, depending on the number of individual panels. These complex wooden forms were often based on Gothic architectural models, sometimes involving ornate forms, and layers of wood glued and nailed together. Larger pieces included battens on the back to prevent them from warping in humid environments, while very large works might be assembled on site. Once the wooden armature was complete, a layer of linen would be pasted down, then covered in gesso to ensure a uniform surface. Painters then painted and gilded these works according to their commission.

Today, you can view works by Tuscan master panel painters like Cimabue and Duccio in the Uffizi Gallery, as well as important works in the churches of Santa Trinita and Santa Maria Novella. While the painters themselves receive credit for their works, most of the carpenters who constructed these elaborate wooden forms usually go unnamed.

So how did the frame become a separate entity apart from a painting? The Florentine Renaissance ushered in the idea of a frame as separate from a painted work, and Florence stood at the epicenter of this transition. In 1423, Palla Strozzi, a banker and at one time the richest man in Florence, commissioned Gentile da Fabriano, a painter who had spent most of his career in Venice, to paint a version of the *Adoration of the Magi*. The gilded panel painting was based on the medieval prototype of an architectural framework, but for the first time, the frame ended up as a separate elaboration from the painting. Over the next decade, other prominent Florentine artists, including Brunelleschi, Donatello, and Michelozzo, contributed to the development of the idea of a frame as a separate work in its own right. As a more classical aesthetic supplanted the Gothic style as the prevailing fashion, frames were a natural outcome.

While painters earned fame and fortune for their works and frame-makers remained largely anonymous, these early frames nonetheless constituted works of extraordinary accomplishment.

WHO MADE DA VINCI'S FRAMES?

As the capital of the Italian Renaissance, Florence is a natural place for the art of frame-making to have taken root. Florentine frame-makers have been in business since painters began to transition from wooden panel paintings to canvas in the fifteenth century, and needed frames to showcase their work. Unfortunately, these master frame-makers did not enjoy the same notoriety as their painter-colleagues such as Botticelli, da Vinci, Massaccio, and others. While many paintings by these Florentine Renaissance masters survive, the wooden frames that originally accompanied them rarely remain with their intended works.

By contrast, today not many artists in Florence claim the same level of accomplishment as Leonardo da Vinci, yet master frame-makers enjoy a flourishing business. The city's many art museums, including the world-class Uffizi Gallery, continue to keep the city's frame-makers and restorers busy, and for visitors, a handmade custom frame is one of the city's best souvenirs.

Frame-makers displayed a remarkable sensitivity to the specific properties of each type of wood. Walnut was prized for its rich color and structural integrity, and was preferred for a frame with fine details, or one that was left to show the wood grain. More inexpensive and softer woods like pine and poplar might be used for less important parts of the frame, less intricate carving, or for areas that would be gilded or painted later in the process.

Although Florentines used a *cassetta* or "box"-style frame that was the same on all four sides, they also made a tabernacle-style frame with an elaborated top and bottom section, as well as the *tondo*, or round frame, popular throughout Tuscany during the Renaissance. Florentine woodworkers drew from classical architecture, vegetal forms, and the decorative vocabulary they already used in carving panels, chests, and other works for interior design.

Lamps and Lighting

Lamps are another creative outlet for those trained in the art of woodcrafting and gilding. Florence is one of the only places in the world where you could have an antique candleholder converted to electricity and order a custom lampshade to fit— even an outrageously ornate, gilded candleholder that stands six feet tall and belongs in a church treasury. That's precisely what one man did while I was waiting in line at a custom lamp maker's shop in the Oltrarno district. This is not surprising, though, when you realize that many of the curvilinear, ornate forms of today's Florentine lamps preserve the memory of antique candelabra made of wood or metal. Florence boasts some of the most unique creations in the world of lighting, and many of these include beautiful wooden forms. Pair them with a handmade, customized lampshade, and you'll go home with a one-of-a-kind Florentine souvenir.

How to Buy Florentine Woodcrafts

Today, a small number of furniture-makers, frame-makers, restorers and other master woodworkers carry on the old Florentine traditions. Although no longer operating in guilds, many traditional woodworkers in Florence remain family affairs. Parents pass the tradition to their children and grand-children, perpetuating the techniques and the spirit of these old works. These families will almost always take the time to educate you about their techniques and history, and answer your questions.

HOW MUCH TO PAY

Several factors can influence the price of a handmade work of wood:

- Portable items such as small frames, sconces, and ornaments are some of the best-kept secrets in Florentine shopping. These items tend to be portable, affordable, high-quality, authentically Florentine, and totally handmade.

- Wooden lamps are also a great value considering the quality and uniqueness. With a small modification by your local lamp shop, the lamp should work just fine in your home country.

- Furniture will set you back much more money. You must also take into account the cost of shipping. Small accent pieces are more affordable and more portable, but prices climb for larger or custom works. Florentine artisans are masters of customization, so if you are looking for a piece made to your specifications, Florentine carpenters are the perfect ones to ask.

- Florence boasts many antique shops with beautiful works of wood. You'll pay top price for these items. You should know what you're doing if you buy an antique. What documentation do you have of the work's provenance? What is the item's origin and state of preservation? Has it been restored and if so, how? Has it been appraised? How will you get it home? How will you insure it? If you are a lover of antique furniture, you will undoubtedly find something in Florence to pull at your heartstrings.

Furniture making requires space and is a relatively messy craft. It's not always possible to watch furniture makers work, as their studios are tucked away from the more slickly merchandized streets of the city, and they require more space than the small *botteghe* in the artisan quarter of the Oltrarno. The makers and restorers of frames, as well as smaller wooden items, are more accessible in this part of town. These items are more portable, and not as prone to breaking as a work of glass or ceramic, so a small, handmade wooden souvenir from Florence is a great choice.

3

Jewelry & Works of Precious Metal

For as far back in history as we can trace, Florentines have loved to adorn themselves with precious metals and gems. Florentine jewelry has held a centuries-old reputation as some of the most finely wrought and beautiful in the world. Throughout the Middle Ages and the Renaissance, local patrons as well as foreign visitors supported dozens of Florentine masters of gold and precious stones.

As much as the work of Florentine jewelers was highly valued, however, it was also tightly regulated. During the Renaissance, the Republic of Florence already controlled many of the professional and personal activities of members of their famous trade guilds. The strict guild statutes of the *orafi* (goldsmiths) and *gioellieri* (jewelers) governed many aspects of these makers' daily lives, covering everything from the materials they used in their work, to the prohibition of imitation gems, to the litigation of disputes among colleagues and customers.

In addition to the guild regulations, makers of jewelry were also bound by sumptuary laws that were intended to prevent displays that Catholic authorities considered sinfully extravagant.

Goldsmiths and jewelers belonged to the *Arte della Seta,* or the silkmakers' guild, because the objects they made—buttons, belts, clasps, and similar works—were considered part of dressmaking. Because of this association with clothing, they fell under strict and specific sumptuary restrictions. These fascinating glimpses into the mentality of fifteenth-century Florentines include examples like this one, plucked from a 1415 statute:

> **a woman cannot wear on one or more fingers more than a total of three rings. And across all the rings and fingers she may not have more than one pearl or another precious stone. These restrictions apply to both hands.**

Florentine city officials could search the premises of a goldsmith or jeweler's shop to ensure that they were not making restricted items for local consumption, under pain of confiscation or fine. Needless to say, for a jeweler working in Renaissance Florence, creating work for the local market must have felt constraining. Their creative talents were put to work instead for the export market, where they were free to craft incredibly intricate flights of fancy: small bees, birds, frogs, plants, tiny ships and castles, and other breathtaking work, since the local sumptuary laws did not bind goldsmiths from making extravagant work for export. A look at some of the production for foreign markets shows that in contrast to what they produced for local clients, these artists let their imaginations run wild.

For their local customers, many Florentine goldsmiths made their bread and butter by crafting engagement rings— simple gold bands. These rings formed the focal point of a special ring ceremony called *l'annellamento* that accompanied Florentine engagements. In this traditional betrothal event, the fiancé placed the ring on the finger of his bride-to-be in the presence of her parents and other family members, making their intentions public.

In addition to rings, bracelets, necklaces, and earrings, many works of Florentine jewelers were meant to be incorporated into clothing: pearls used in embroidered headwear, glass beads or gilded tinsel sewn onto cuffs and collars, and precious stones incorporated into buttons, lace, or other fine trims. Necklines were frequently embellished with copper, gold, enamel, floral, and vegetal forms, and were of particular concern for sumptuary law officials. Women are frequently named in historical documents as the makers of clothing ornamentation, involving the production of copper and gold wire, and beating sheets of silver and gold. The complex vocabulary that developed to describe the various types of clothing ornaments confused even those trying to make and regulate them. One can quickly become lost in the terminology used in historical chronicles, inventories, and statutes describing such finery.

Another group of specialized craftspeople occupied themselves with working precious metals in the service of the church, churning out reliquaries, censers, and other church furnishings and liturgical objects.

According to the poet and historian Benedetto Dei, who celebrated the glories of his native city in a work entitled *Florentie bella* in the 1470s, Florence counted some forty-four jewelers and thirty-three gold and silver shops at that time. About half of the goldsmiths were clustered in the neighborhood around the church of Santo Spirito. Other goldsmiths and also those specializing in

---

RENAISSANCE MEN

Did you know? Some of the most renowned artists of the Florentine Renaissance—including Botticelli and Donatello—began their training as apprentices to goldsmiths.

gemstone jewelry occupied the streets surrounding the churches of Santa Maria Novella and San Giovanni.

By the end of the sixteenth century, though, the Ponte Vecchio would come to be associated with goldsmiths. The Ponte Vecchio–the "Old Bridge"–of Florence is the oldest bridge in the city. Both a commercial space as well as a major thoroughfare, the Ponte Vecchio has been a place to browse, barter, and people-watch for more than six hundred years. The bridge has hosted shops since its construction in the fourteenth century. Florentines have constructed, reconstructed, renovated, and added onto the commercial buildings on the bridge over that time, and today these structures present a fascinating conglomeration of colors, styles, and functions.

Until the thirteenth century, the Ponte Vecchio was the only way to cross the Arno. The current structure was built between 1339 and 1346, connecting the Piazza della Repubblica with the Oltrarno district. Shops appeared on the bridge immediately, as it was common practice during the Middle Ages for certain types of businesses to cluster on bridges. Early on, butchers occupied most of the shops on the Ponte Vecchio, so that they could conveniently dispose of their waste by chucking it into the Arno River below.

Things changed, though, under the ruling Medici family. In 1549, Cosimo I de Medici moved into the Palazzo Pitti, on the south side of the Arno. Every day the Medici entourage walked to their offices on the north side of the Arno, located in what is now the Uffizi Gallery (*uffizi* means "offices" in Tuscan dialect). According to the story, Cosimo grew squeamish at the sights and smells of the butcher shops on the bridge he passed each day, and decided that it was time for a change. He gave the butchers six months' notice, and replaced the tenants with goldsmiths instead. While on the surface this may seem like an upgrade, the location of goldsmiths on the bridge may still have had an olfactory motive, as the smell of the sulfur used in the gilding process could waft down the Arno and away from the city center. But the Medici had a

SHOPPING THE PONTE VECCHIO

Today the Ponte Vecchio is known for gold jewelry merchants who cater to a lucrative tourist trade. For that reason, prices are set accordingly high, and I don't recommend buying here. With a few exceptions, many of the sparkling items in the windows are not handmade, and unfortunately some may not have been made in Florence. Still, strolling the bridge and window-shopping are an integral part of the Florentine experience, so don't miss it! When you're ready to buy, scout out the handful of less well-known artisan jewelers, in the Oltrarno and on the streets just north of the bridge, where everything is made by hand.

greater effect on the history of Florentine jewelry than making the Ponte Vecchio the epicenter of production. It was their patronage of Florentine gold- and silversmiths that propelled Florentine jewelry and metalworking to everlasting fame.

How Florentine Jewelry is Made

In the 1570s, the Florentine goldsmith Benvenuto Cellini wrote a treatise about goldsmithing that describes some of the techniques used at that time. Cellini's own production included the famous *saliera* or salt-cellar, now in the Kunsthistorisches Museum in Vienna, that Cellini made for the Cardinal Ippolito d'Este. Cellini was just one of many accomplished masters of precious metals in the city, however. The gold, bronze, and silver objects in the Medici collection at the Pitti Palace bear witness to the technical excellence of which Florentine metalsmiths were capable at that time. Today's artisanal goldsmiths in Florence keep many of these same techniques alive.

In a densely populated city like medieval and Renaissance Florence, workers of precious metals occupied cramped spaces, often small studios within or attached to their homes. They hunched over narrow workbenches with various drawers for tools and fabric pouches or "catches" to hold tools and dropped items, which might be hot. A small slab of charcoal, which retained heat, provided the primary workspace, heated with an open flame from an oil lamp.

No matter what the technique or desired result, working precious metals began with heating them in order to make them malleable. Working at such a small scale and in close proximity to their work, jewelers had to come up with ways to heat metal with a small heat source. The invention of the foot bellows allowed a jeweler to work at a small bench and control the airflow to a flame with some precision. Today, contemporary jewelers use a small flame from a blowtorch. Goldsmiths often hammered, flattened, or otherwise formed a piece while the metal was in this molten state. Florentine jewelers of centuries past also used a variety of metal forms and shapes that aided them in forming a particular piece into the shape they wanted.

Jewelers worked with a variety of stones, files, and buffers to achieve particular effects, as well as a foot-powered wheel to grind away or file hard edges. Their workbenches also included various liquid and powdered chemicals (borax, sulfur, potash, lime, or other materials) used to form, bind, and add color to metals. These chemicals, along with the open flame the artisans needed to soften metal, posed certain occupational hazards.

The most important tool in the jeweler's arsenal, however, had to be eyeglasses. Eyeglasses first appeared in the Western world in Tuscany, where they are mentioned in a Pisan document dating from 1286. The availability of magnification surely allowed jewelers to achieve greater intricacy and precision in their work and also allowed jewelers to work in the trade for more years than they might have otherwise.

Florentine Jewelry Techniques

Many of the finest works of Florentine jewelry can only be described as sculpture in miniature. It would be easy to fill an entire book with terminology and techniques related to the making of jewelry in precious metals. Florentine goldsmithing is a complex art with many different techniques and combinations, as well as a rich history. Without diving too deeply

into the technical details, here are some of the main types of precious metalworking that you will come to recognize if you take the time to look carefully.

Filigree

The word *filigree* joins together two Latin roots, *filium* ("thread") and *granum* ("grain"), which describes the technique in a nutshell. Filigree involves twisting threads of silver or gold, and/or adhering tiny beads to achieve a granulated surface. The goldsmith may twist, curl, or braid fine wires into a pattern, connecting separate pieces by heating them with a flame from a blowpipe, and joining them with flux (one or more chemical agents used in jewelry making). Granulation involves soldering together miniscule metal beads, sometimes on a flat metal surface. Filigree was used widely in antiquity, as far back as the ancient Mesopotamian and Egyptian civilizations. In Renaissance Florence, metalsmiths often employed filigree to embellish headpieces, as seen in many portraits of the era.

Niello

Niello involves using copper, silver, lead, or sulfur as a black background for intricate designs engraved on the metal surface. The technique is closely aligned with engraving, and was used as far back as ancient Egypt. Niello was widely employed in Renaissance Florence, not only in jewelry, but especially in the making of buckles, book bindings, suits of armor, and infinite varieties of liturgical works found in church treasuries.

Enamel

In jewelry, enamelling involves fusing molten glass to a surface, which hardens to a smooth coating often with deep, saturated color. Enamel is usually opaque but can sometimes have levels of transparency and can also be combined with metal oxides to achieve different effects. Enamel has been used since the days of ancient Rome. In medieval and Renaissance Florence, jewelers commonly used red and blue vitreous enamels to create vegetal and floral patterns against a gold or silver ground.

Cameos and intaglio

In jewelry, intaglio refers to engraving or cutting an image into the flat background of a gemstone such as sardonyx or carnelian. Conversely, cameos involve relief carvings, or designing an image to project out of a background composed of a gem or seashell cut with small hand tools and abrasive or powdered stones. Although cameos and engraved gemstones were popular among the ancient Greeks and Romans, the Medici family's patronage brought a renewed taste for engraved gems to Florence in the sixteenth century. The family cultivated an extensive private collection of gems from antiquity, and prompted jewelers in town to replicate these ancient designs.

Precious stones

During the Middle Ages and the Renaissance, Europeans appreciated sapphires, rubies, garnets, and emeralds in their own right, and Florentine jewelers' guild statutes prohibited them from using imitation gemstones. To highlight the beauty of these precious stones, the metalsmithing that went along with them remained relatively understated. Pearls were among the most popular precious stones, worn as jewelry but also commonly used in embroidery to embellish collars, cuffs, headdresses, and buttons. They were also used in hairnets and to stud more elaborate hairstyles.

How to Buy Florentine Jewelry

Gold is measured in karats, indicating the amount of pure gold that constitutes a piece of jewelry. Twenty-four karats (24k) designates gold in its purest state. However, twenty-four-karat gold is too soft to be used in jewelry making. By mixing pure gold with other alloys such as silver or copper, it can be worked by a jeweler. An eighteen-karat gold ring contains seventy-five percent pure gold. In other words, it contains eighteen parts gold and six parts another metal or metals. This information is important when pricing gold jewelry in Florence, since some jewelers sell gold jewelry based on weight alone, tagging the price of their work to the varying values in the gold market.

In the U.S., ten karats is the lowest legal standard at which a piece of jewelry can be referred to as "gold," though fourteen-karat gold is the most popular. In Italy, however, eighteen karats is the lowest legal standard to carry the label "gold." This higher percentage of gold helps explain why gold jewelry in Italy seems more brilliant and also softer. This preference for more "pure" gold goes back to antiquity, as the ancient Romans preferred to use a more unadulterated form of brilliant gold as a raw material for jewelry.

By combining gold with different metals such as copper and silver, jewelers can achieve different coloration. In Florence, you will see different shades of gold combined together. Rose gold (*oro rosa*) is achieved by combining gold with copper. White gold (*oro bianco*) combines gold with copper, nickel, and zinc. Yellow gold (*oro giallo*) combines gold with copper and silver.

Though you may not ultimately buy there, a trip to Florence would not be complete without a stroll across the beautiful Ponte Vecchio while window-shopping for gold jewelry. As you make your way across the historic bridge, be sure to pay attention to the

complex wooden shuttering mechanisms used to lock the store-fronts at night. Although these wooden and iron contraptions have been constructed in relatively recent times, they bear close resemblance to shuttering mechanisms depicted in prints and paintings of the fifteenth and sixteenth centuries. Medieval and Renaissance gold merchants once lifted these shutters to provide protection from the elements, both for the seller and the merchandise displayed on the counter. At the same time, the complex system of locks and imposing-looking heavy shutters dissuaded thieves from trying to break in to steal valuable inventory when the shutters were battened down after hours.

Today, a walk across the bridge allows us to experience what most bridges in the 1400s must have been like: places to browse, barter, people-watch, or consider an offer that may prove difficult to refuse. Things have not changed much. Now, as then, it's a good idea to watch your wallet while strolling the bridge, as the Ponte Vecchio has a centuries-old reputation for people-watching opportunities, alluring window shopping, and the occasional swindle.

HOW MUCH TO PAY

Prices for Florentine jewelry vary according to three main factors:

- The weight of the gold, priced according to the fluctuating market values of precious metals.

- The techniques used to execute the piece. Expect to pay more for custom and intricate designs.

- The repute of the maker, especially if you buy from one of the famous brands like Milanese jewelry house Buccellati, which command higher prices because of the cachet behind their names.

4

Leather Goods

I n Florence, leather shopping can amount to an obsession. Some city streets and squares overflow with handbags, jackets, belts, wallets, and countless other accessories synonymous with Made-in-Italy quality and style. For many international travelers to Florence, leather shopping is on the top of their to-do list as the city carries a worldwide reputation for these goods.

Leather working in Florence is a centuries-old trade involving craftspeople of many types: makers of apparel such as aprons, shoes, and belts; of leather book bindings; and of Florentine military outfitting for men and horses. Some leather workers specialized in making chest plates, collaborating with metalsmiths to construct suits of armor, scabbards, saddles, and elaborate horse tack for the Republic's military troops.

Prior to the Industrial Revolution, preparing animal hides to make leather was considered particularly unsavory work. Not only did tanning hides involve backbreaking physical labor, but the tanneries (*conciatori*) themselves were famous for their foul odors and grim working conditions. Tanners began by loosening animal fur from the hides and soaking the pelts in a solution of lime and other substances, which, in addition to the processing of animal carcasses, contributed to the stench. Ultimately, every bit of hair had to be removed by beating the hides and scraping them with knives and other special tools (our word "pelting" comes from this trade). Tanners then stretched the pelts on vertical wooden racks so that the hides could dry and season in the sun. In medieval Florence, many of the tanneries were located along the Arno in order to facilitate washing away the detritus of this process, and in many other cities of medieval Europe the tanneries were required to locate outside the city walls altogether. The via dei Conciatori, in the eastern part of the city near Santa Croce, retains the memory of the Florentine tanneries and is the location of the current Scuola del Cuoio or leather school.

Although they remained of modest means, shoemakers sat atop the leather hierarchy and were considered a pillar of medieval Florentine society. By the 1300s some 1,500 shoemakers were already working in the city. About a third of these settled in the Oltrarno district. Cobblers made shoes for local consumption, but also participated in a lively export trade, forming the roots of the Tuscan international leather shoe industry that still thrives today. The statutes of the shoemakers' guild or *Arte dei Calzaiuoli* (or *Calzolai*) specified many aspects of their working lives, from the quality and types of leather that the shoemakers must use in their production, down to their shop opening hours. Fifteenth-century documents place shoe- and belt-makers' shops along the via dei Calzaiuoli, as well as on the streets stretching toward the church of Santo Stefano near the Ponte Vecchio. In contrast to the high-end fashion boutiques that line the via dei Calzaiuoli today, surely this street must have been lined instead with more humble workshops.

In addition to apparel, leather specialists across the city plied their trades in the production of parchment sheets, closely linked to the bookbinding trade (see Chapter 6). Medieval and Renaissance manuscripts relied on parchment paper made from cured sheepskins; if you look closely at a medieval manuscript folio you can see the pores! Leather covers were crafted to protect the books and provide a luxurious and beautiful exterior. Leather workers also pioneered techniques for armor and ceremonial dress and worked with saddle and tack makers to create horse regalia for ceremonial and everyday use.

Florence held a reputation for its quality leather production for hundreds of years, but in the early twentieth century, the industry was propelled to new heights. A Florentine named Guccio Gucci, son of a leather artisan, turned his back on the family business as a young man. Working in a series of menial jobs at the Savoy Hotel in London, he carried stylish pieces of luggage for wealthy visitors. Gucci returned home to Florence in 1921 and began turning his family trade to designing high-end leather luggage and accessories for a wealthy international clientele. He soon propelled the leather goods of his native city to international fame as one of the most recognized names in the fashion world. Since World War II, leather has become one of Italy's most important economic sectors and Florence has retained its reputation for world-class quality leather goods.

How Leather is Made

Today, the tanning and working of leather is much more complicated than it was in the days of those malodorous medieval tanneries that dotted the Arno. In fact, the production and marketing of leather products in Italy is an extraordinarily complex topic that touches culture, history, fashion, economy, and the very core of Italian self-identity. In order to grasp this complex world of Italian leather today, it helps to think about the industry as divided into three tiers: industrial, luxury-branded, and artisanal.

The largest of these sectors is the industrial, employing tens of thousands of workers and representing a major force in Italy's domestic and export economies. Many of the Italian leather jackets, purses, belts, gloves, and shoes carried in chic apparel shops around the world are produced in enterprises concentrated outside of Florence and Milan. In recent years, the relatively high cost of Italian leather and competition with Asian imports have presented new challenges to Italian leather makers, yet leather remains an important part of the Italian economy and cultural identity as it exemplifies the concept of "Made in Italy" for many international consumers.

Animal hides are still sourced from Italy today, but also from elsewhere in Europe and abroad. Many of the hides are prepared in small to medium-sized firms across Tuscany, with a concentration of such companies scattered between Florence and Pisa, notably in Santa Croce sull'Arno and Ponte a Egola. Firms near Florence and Milan also produce most of the machinery used in industrial leather production, including those used in the tanning process; in the assembly of shoes, bags, and apparel; and in the processing of leather for the automotive and furniture industries. These companies prepare and assemble hides with special machines and chemicals, with a wide variety of processing methods and quality. The majority of the leather apparel made in Italy today is produced in this more industrial setting, and within it, the Italian shoe industry is a world unto itself. Many of the items you see in the leather shops or *pelletterie* of Florence were made in these medium-sized industrial enterprises in the Tuscan countryside, and distributed to the shops via wholesalers.

The second tier is the production of leather intended for resale in the boutiques of some of the most recognized Italian luxury brand names in the international fashion world. Here's where things get complicated, since much of the perceived value of the luxury leather brands lies in the selection and treatment of the raw materials, as well as in the craftsmanship behind each finished piece. A few luxury companies produce everything in their own factories, allowing for tighter control over the handling of materials and quality of work. However, most subcontract at least some aspects of production to those companies in the industrial sector—the same ones who are making leather for cars and sofas, for example. They may outsource the procurement and preparation of hides, as well as the cutting and stitching of bags, jackets, skirts, dresses, gloves, and other items. On the other hand, most of the luxury brands also make sure that certain signature items are hand-finished in house. They employ skilled artisans to complete these hand-finished details, and readily employ images of the leather workers in their marketing materials. For the most part, it's accurate to view these luxury-branded items as a hybrid of industrial and artisanal production, as the fundamental business of these luxury companies relies on selling well-made, high-quality products on a large scale.

JUDGING LEATHER QUALITY

Imagine that you could take an animal hide and examine a cross-section of it under a microscope. At the top layer, you would see the pores of the skin, scars and imperfections, hair follicles, and the hairs themselves. Directly beneath, you would find thick, densely woven tissue with many overlapping fibers. Below that, you would see another layer of fibers, less dense and laid out in a more horizontal pattern. Today, most hides go through special machines that skim off each of these individual layers. Determining leather quality is based on what happens next:

Full-grain (*pieno fiore*): Full-grain leather is considered the best that money can buy. It represents the top layer of the hide, and has usually not been sanded, so that you can still see scars, imperfections, and pores. Full-grain leather is considered desirable for its supple texture and durability, natural aroma, and its ability to take on a beautiful patina over time. The key term to look for is *pieno fiore* (*cuoio pieno fiore* or *pelle pieno fiore*).

Top-grain (*parte grano* or *cuoio di grano*): Top-grain leather showcases that densely packed grain or patterning of the top layer of the pelt, but it has been sanded to remove some of the imperfections. Sometimes Italians don't make strict distinctions between full-grain and top-grain leather, so there can remain some ambiguity even though top-grain leather is still considered very high quality in Italy.

Genuine (*vera pelle* or *vero cuoio*): Genuine leather is cut from the bottom half of the hide and reveals no grain even though it may still be supple, rich in color, and retain a pleasant aroma. Suede is an example of genuine leather.

Bonded (*cuoio rigenerato*): Bonded leather results from the detritus of the leather-making process—leather dust, shavings, and excess pieces—that have been swept up and pressed together in the factory with the aid of various chemicals, dyes, and glues. Be careful: bonded leather is often spray painted to resemble natural leather grain. Your nose will tell you whether the piece smells like a cow or Superglue.

Imitation: If you want authentic leather, steer clear of *simipelle* (imitation leather). However, *ecopelle* (a more appealing-sounding name for the same thing) might be a more attractive solution for those who do not wear animal products at all.

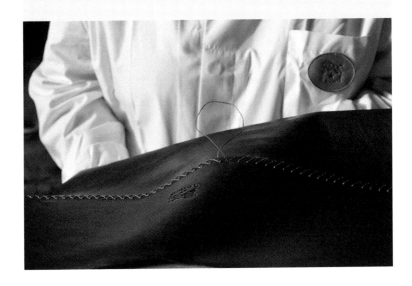

Last but not least are the individual artisanal leather producers. Florence boasts many of these unsung masters of leather, and it's worth the effort to seek them out for their beautiful pieces, as well as the opportunity to watch them work. Here the focus is less on the preparation of hides and more on the craftsmanship of cutting, fitting, sewing, stitching, and hand-finishing a custom work. Today, fully handcrafted leather production in Florence focuses on bookbinding and the making of small objects such as boxes and desk sets. There are, however, a handful of leather artisans making gloves, shoes, bags, and other fashion accessories completely by hand.

How to Buy Florentine Leather

Today, the opportunities to buy leather in Florence are vast, from luxury boutiques, to raucous street bazaars, to "private" workshops, to sidewalk trinket sellers. To make matters more confusing, things are rarely what they seem on the surface. You

can find a reasonably priced bag on the street whose quality equals an item in a high-end boutique. Other times, the same merchant may sell the same bag in a *pelletteria* and also in a market stall, at two very different prices. Some pieces are made on an industrial scale, others on an artisanal one, and sometimes the same merchant may sell both.

If you're serious about going home with a quality leather souvenir, you should know a few tricks of the Florentine leather-shopping trade. First, if you can buy directly from the maker, that's the absolute best guarantee of knowing exactly what you're buying. However, in Florence buying leather directly from an artisan is only easy when buying small, portable items like boxes, wallets, and change purses. Most apparel items are sold in small retail shops. In this case, *what* you buy is more important than *where* you buy. Try to divorce the handbag or jacket from its setting if you can and focus instead on the quality of the individual piece.

The San Lorenzo market attracts leather-shopping visitors from Tokyo to Tulsa, with its pulsating rhythm, the chatter of bargaining merchants, the bustle of the crowd, and the musky

MADE TO MEASURE

For a pair of handcrafted custom shoes, would you be willing to wait four months and pay four times what you would pay in an average shoe store? In my experience, the answer is yes for many travelers, especially if they've selected one of Florence's wonderful artisanal shoemakers. If you are in the market for a pair of handmade shoes, Florence boasts unparalleled opportunities to not only go home with a beautiful pair of shoes made just for you, but also to make a connection with the person whose labor and passion went into crafting it.

aroma of leather wafting into the air. The market itself includes an indoor section known as the Mercato Centrale, which sells mostly food items, while the outdoor market is known for leather. You will not necessarily find the lowest prices or the best quality here, but I have still scored some good-quality finds, including a classic brown jacket I bought a decade ago that still looks great. Many of these street vendors also operate retail stores. Their street-side stalls are just another venue for generating sales, without the over-head of a shop. That's how you might find the same item with two or more different prices.

Another popular leather-shopping spot is the Mercato Nuovo, also known as the "*porcellino*" market for the bronze pig whose nose has been rubbed smooth by superstitious travelers to guarantee a future trip to Florence. During the Renaissance, wealthy Florentines shopped for gold and silk under the arcades of this beautiful marketplace. Later, it became known for straw vendors. Today, leather takes center stage in the Mercato Nuovo. As in the San Lorenzo market, quality and price vary widely. This is one of the trickiest places to shop in Florence, so be sure to use your skills of distinguishing higher from lower quality in order to ensure you make a purchase you'll still be happy about when you get home.

Bargaining is the norm in the markets and I have found that you can easily take off ten to twenty percent simply by asking, or by plying some tried-and-true haggling techniques such as offering to pay cash, buying more than one item at the same time, or just walking away. Talented hagglers might get the price down to half. In shops, bargaining is less common and usually less successful, but it never hurts to ask.

One of the market vendors may extend you an "exclusive invitation" to visit their "private" leather workshop. Yes, these are mostly gimmicks geared toward making tourists think they're getting the deal of a lifetime. Here's how it works: You follow a high-pressure salesman (truthfully, it's usually a charming,

HOW JUDGE QUALITY LEATHER

When it comes to judging leather quality, try to forget whether you're in a bustling street market or a high-end boutique. Instead, let the buying environment fade out of focus, and use your senses:

Aroma: When it comes to judging leather, follow your nose. The item should smell musky and natural. Steer clear of anything that smells like chemicals, which are used to treat the hides and cover up lesser quality. Your sense of smell and touch will help determine the quality of the leather. The more supple the leather feels, the better. If an acrid, chemical smell assaults you when you enter the shop, chances are the goods are heavily dyed to disguise lesser-quality bonded leather. A wonderful, earthy aroma characterizes natural leather.

Suppleness: The leather should feel smooth, supple, and soft, not stiff.

Color: The highest quality natural leather in tan or brown can stand on its own, without any added color, to reveal the natural grain and beauty of the material. Dyes, in red or green, for example, can mask lesser quality leather. If the edges of the leather are unfinished, you should be able to tell if the color lies on the surface or penetrates all the way through the hide. If you buy a blue bag, for example, you may only see blue on the surface, not in the middle. If that's the case, chances are, this is bonded leather whose surface has been sprayed with dye, perhaps to resemble a grain-like "natural" pattern.

Stitching and other details: The stitching should be tight and regular, with small stitches sewn close together. Silk or satin lining is used in higher-quality bags and apparel.

STREET BAGS

Whatever you do, do not buy a "brand name" handbag in Florence from someone selling it on a blanket spread out on the sidewalk. This advice may seem like common sense, but tantalizingly cheap prices lure visitors into this trap every day. For Italian authorities, this scam is considered serious business, as the brand-name leather trade is a major driver of the Italian economy. In recent decades, authorities have cracked down with greater force on vendors selling knockoff bags to buyers who either don't know the difference or are more than happy with a low-priced imitation. I have seen women purchase handbags on the street, only to turn around and have to hand over the bags directly to uniformed *carabinieri* waiting for the transaction to close. These customers do not get their money back; it's just not worth it.

handsome Italian man) to an unmarked door down a side street. There you encounter a no-frills warehouse-type setting chock full of leather apparel, and perhaps a few more handsome Florentines. They'll help you try on jackets before a mirror, all the while asking if *all* American women are as beautiful as you. Impressive sales tactics, no doubt.

What you pay depends mostly on where you buy. I priced a popular type of medium-sized shoulder bag in several places around the city. A street vendor near Santa Croce carried the style I wanted and I bargained him down to about thirty-five percent off the original asking price, but the stitching was beginning to fray and the leather felt stiff, so I passed. A similarly styled bag in a high-end boutique near the Duomo—this one of great quality with soft leather, silk lining, and fine stitching—was exorbitantly priced. In the end, I found a winner, the quality equal to the higher-priced bag, in an unassuming boutique on a less-trafficked street. This experience is typical of Florentine leather shopping. Some visitors find the experience confusing or exasperating, while others relish the thrill of the hunt.

As a general rule, Florentine leather goods are not cheap, but often represent a good value considering the quality. The safest bet is to buy directly from the maker and to focus on small, portable items—boxes, change purses, eyeglass cases, albums, desk accessories—rather than apparel, which is more complex and tricky to get right. Many of these small items are completely handmade on site, and the prices are typically reasonable. They also make durable souvenirs and special gifts that are either easy to transport in your suitcase or relatively simple to ship.

5

Maiolica Ceramics

When most people think of Italian ceramics, they think of maiolica: the rich, colorful tin-glazed earthenware that flourished in the fourteenth, fifteenth, and sixteenth centuries in ceramics towns across the Italian peninsula. In central Italy, however, ceramics represent much more than objects with aesthetic value. Clay vessels formed an economic backbone for the region for some five centuries and today maiolica retains a position as one of central Italy's finest examples of cultural patrimony.

Merchants began unloading large numbers of Spanish ceramic wares from their ships in Italian port cities around 1360. Italians immediately appreciated the aesthetic qualities of these Spanish imports, with their white background and bright colors. In fact, they were willing to pay more for these shiny, reflective wares than they were the plainer, utilitarian ceramic vessels made locally. The demand for lustrous Spanish wares sparked a competition, and Italians began to innovate in creating these wares themselves. They experimented with new ceramic techniques to impart a shiny white surface and used cobalt oxide to create a bright, saturated blue resembling the highly prized precious stone lapis lazuli. The tradition of Italian maiolica was born.

CERAMICS AND INTERNATIONAL ESPIONAGE

In the 1300s, Florentine ceramics merchants hired spies along the Spanish coast to try to divine how Spanish workshops achieved such shiny, reflective white surfaces and bright, saturated colors. Soon, Italian maiolica was established in its own right and Florence stood at the economic epicenter of the maiolica trade.

By the late Middle Ages, ceramic families on hilltop villages across the Tuscan and Umbrian countryside worked with merchants and exporters in what constituted a major international industry. Many thousands of vessels were exported to London, Amsterdam, Constantinople, and beyond. Ceramic-making families competed with one another, closely guarding their secrets.

Although Florentine merchants played a central role in the international ceramics economy, maiolica production was limited in Florence itself because a fear of fire kept the ceramics trade, with its hot kilns, outside of the city. A handful of potters were working in the Oltrarno district in the late Middle Ages, probably supplying the population with utilitarian wares for everyday use, such as plates, cups, bowls, and other vessels.

In the early 1430s, a Florentine potter named Giunta di Tugio broke the mold, so to speak, by making a large collection of maiolica pharmacy jars for the Arcispedale Santa Maria Nuova, the city's most important hospital. Hospital and monastery pharmacies represented major commissions for medieval ceramicists, as pharmacies needed large numbers of jars to hold medicinal concoctions. For Santa Maria Nuova, di Tugio made some one thousand apothecary jars, each bearing the image of a crutch, the emblem of the hospital. The style of the jars—all with bright blue vegetal and limited figural designs against a shiny white background—shows the reliance on examples made in Spain under Islamic influence. At the time, people referred to this style as *a zaffera*. Within the next decade, Luca della Robbia worked on another major commission of maiolica, a series of colored glazed terracotta panels to decorate the exterior of Florence's cathedral. He went on to create a number of works of maiolica for use in architectural settings across Florence.

Apart from a few important commissions like these, the heart of the story of Florentine ceramics lies outside the city. Montelupo Fiorentino, a small town about twenty kilometers to the west of Florence along the Arno, emerged and thrived as a ceramics supplier to Florentine nobles and its rising merchant class. The Florentine government saw Montelupo Fiorentino as a strategic location because the outlying hill town boasted a fortress that had already been in place for centuries. Florence pulled Montelupo into its territories in 1204, rebuilding the castle and enlarging the town's walls.

Starting between 1360 and 1380, when the "new maiolica" began to be produced in greater numbers in Tuscany, a group of ceramics masters established kilns in Montelupo Fiorentino. The Medici family eventually built a country villa on the left bank of the Arno in Montelupo, and nearby land would be procured by other prominent Florentine families, including the Antinori, Frescobaldi, Mannelli, Spina, Strozzi, and Ambrogi. Montelupo quickly thrived on the fortunes of their Florentine customers, composed of this group of nobles who had established country estates there, as well as an increasingly wealthy merchant class in the city.

FEAR AND THE "FIRE ARTS"

The danger of fire outbreaks was so great in medieval cities that the "fire arts"—ceramics and glass—usually took place on the outskirts or in smaller towns. That's why there were not many kilns in Florence itself, and the maiolica masters of Montelupo Fiorentino, just outside the city, were able to build a lively trade. They profited from being able to ship their ceramic wares along the Arno River to Florence, where these colorful ceramics were snapped up by local customers and exported as far afield as Constantinople.

This wealthy audience commissioned ceramic masters to create individual pieces and entire table services to commemorate engagements, marriages, political alliances, business deals, friendship, and more. Florentines commissioned ceramics artists from Montelupo Fiorentino to provide a steady flow of commemorative vases with coats of arms to mark important political relationships between families. They tasked ceramics masters with creating "his-and-hers" plates depicting the elegant profiles of a bride and groom. They covered their tables with brightly painted wares depicting themes of hunting, mythology, and heraldry. The economic and demographic dynamics of Florence in the fifteenth and sixteenth centuries made this period the heyday of ceramic production in Montelupo.

The turn of the fifteenth century marked an important time in the history of ceramics in Montelupo. In 1406, the Florentines won a military battle over their rivals in Pisa, which opened the route to Italy's western ports and the sea. The ceramics of Montelupo Fiorentino were transported on small boats down the Arno River and then to the trading ports of Pisa and Livorno, where they were exported around the Mediterranean on merchant ships. Florence quickly dominated trade across the Mediterranean in the early decades of the fifteenth century, having taken over many of Pisa's commercial activities, including both ceramics production and commercial shipping. The boats also traveled northward, and the ceramics of Montelupo Fiorentino found eager buyers in London and Amsterdam.

A small group of ceramics families living inside the fortified walls of Montelupo Fiorentino flourished during these decades, regularly loading riverboats with their wares. Smaller villages outside of Montelupo, including the town of Bacchereto, also profited from this bustling international trade. We can grasp the enormity of the industry in a notary deed of 1490, in which the Florentine Francesco Antinori engaged twenty-three potters in Montelupo Fiorentino to supply him exclusively with their

MAIOLICA OR MAJOLICA?

Florentine documents from the Middle Ages and the Renaissance are filled with a dizzying array of terms to describe ceramic wares. Sometimes they describe vessels by their type (pharmacy jars, pitchers, and so on). Other times, they indicate a particular style (Damaschino, for example), or use a more vague stylistic term such as a *zaffera* or a *lustro* to refer to the characteristic lustrous, shiny surface effects.

Up until the sixteenth century the more generalized term *maiolica* was used to describe works of Spanish origin, but eventually it came to designate Italian tin-glazed earthenware as well. One theory is that the word *maiolica* derived from the Spanish term *obra de málequa*, or "work from Málaga," a reference to an important Spanish ceramic center. Another idea is that "maiolica" is how Tuscans would have pronounced Majorca, the island off the Spanish coast from which many of these early works of tin-glazed earthenware came into Italy. (In a similar way, the French word *faïence* is based on a linguistic adaptation of Faenza, another Italian town famous for its ceramic tradition).

To make matters even more confusing, in the mid-nineteenth century, a group of ceramicists in Stoke-on-Trent, England, began producing a class of tableware, tile, and art pieces with a clear, lustrous glaze. They marketed these works as "majolica" even though from a stylistic point of view, they bore little in common with the continental works bearing a similar name. In any case, the "j" spelling caught on in English-speaking countries, and the word *majolica* became slightly more common in English while *maiolica* was more frequently used in other languages.

Today, you will see the terms *maiolica* and *majolica* used interchangeably to describe Italian tin-glazed earthenware. Instead of getting bogged down in the differences, it's important to realize that the two terms probably derive from the same idea and linguistic root. Whether you use maiolica or majolica, these words remain a simpler way to describe these ceramic works rather than the more technically accurate term, "tin-glazed earthenware."

entire production of "general," "Damaschino," and "Vantaggino"-style wares for three years. At the end of those three years, Antinori shipped some 6,300 pieces of these ceramic wares to Constantinople!

By the early sixteenth century ceramics production in Montelupo Fiorentino began to decline because of competition from other Italian centers like Faenza and Urbino, as well as turmoil in the Florentine economy. Montelupo was hit by a series of plagues in the early seventeenth century, causing the ceramics industry to decline further.

When Asian porcelain came into vogue in the second half of the seventeenth century, wealthy classes of Europeans snapped up Dutch imitations of Chinese export porcelain and they began to view maiolica as old-fashioned. In the nineteenth century, the old maiolica tradition enjoyed a brief revival, incorporating more ornate Victorian—and then Art Nouveau—tastes into its stylistic vocabulary.

In 1973 an archeological excavation in Montelupo revealed a *pozzo dei lavatoi* (washerwomens' well) with hundreds of ceramic shards—discards from the kilns within the castle wall—encased within it. Subsequent excavations have revealed other significant finds from the Renaissance. These important discoveries have helped redefine the role of Montelupo Fiorentino within the history of ceramics, as prior to that time Montelupo's important place as a ceramics center had not been fully understood. Since the 1970s, ceramics artists in Montelupo have focused on reproducing the designs and colors of the Renaissance, and also pushing the tradition into new directions.

In addition to the better-known maiolica legacy of the Renaissance, two additional ceramic traditions in the Florentine sphere deserve note. In 1737, the Marchese Ginori founded a porcelain factory in Doccia, about twenty kilometers northeast of Florence. At that time, Chinese export porcelain was popular with European nobles, and many porcelain works were founded in Europe to attempt to replicate the delicate, translucent effects of porcelain. From 1896, the Doccia factory became known as Richard-Ginori. In that same year, Galileo Chini founded an important ceramic manufactory known as Arte della Ceramica that contributed to Liberty Style in Italy. Today Arte della Ceramica is still active in Borgo San Lorenzo, northeast of Florence.

How Maiolica is Made

Making maiolica involves layering colored pigments on top of a white glaze achieved with tin oxide. When fired in a kiln, this technique imparts brightly colored, shiny colors that pop from a creamy, opaque background. This bold contrast of color against the white, along with characteristic stylistic conventions based on a visual vocabulary of the Italian Renaissance, first propelled this

type of ceramic ware to fame and keeps it popular even by today's standards of taste.

We owe our knowledge of early maiolica making to Cipriano Piccolpasso of Casteldurante, whose book *Li tre libri dell'arte del vasaio* (*Three Books on the Potter's Art*), written in the 1550s, details the inner workings of Italian Renaissance ceramics workshops. The illustrated treatise, now in the Victoria and Albert Museum in London, describes everything from the preparation of materials, to the choice of colors, to the firing and decoration of individual pieces. In his dedication, Piccolpasso states that his purpose is to share these masters' heretofore hidden "secrets" with the rest of the world.

Historically, the ceramics workshop operated according to a rigorous hierarchy, with specific jobs for masters, journeymen, and apprentices. Younger assistants were tasked with preparing materials, including the clay, oxides, and pigments, as well as with cleanup. More experienced apprentices might specialize in throwing pots on the wheel. Others with painterly talents may be tasked exclusively with the decoration of vessels. On days when the kiln was fired, workers might suspend their regular work to tend it. In this way they collaborated to ensure a successful firing of the many pieces—perhaps representing weeks of the workshop's production—stacked inside the room-sized oven.

Renaissance-era ceramicists in Montelupo Fiorentino began the process of making vessels by drawing soft clay from nearby fluvial deposits and transporting it via oxcart or water into town. Paradoxically, the Arno itself was viewed as having too many impurities to make its clay ideal, so the river was used primarily for transporting finished wares rather than as a resource for raw material. The clay was often stored in a trough behind the ceramics workshop, kept wet and pliable by one of the workshop assistants. After kneading or wedging the clay to rid it of air pockets that might burst during firing, the piece was thrown on a foot-powered potter's wheel or formed by hand. Pieces removed from the potter's wheel or work surface were left to dry. Next, the pieces were stacked into the kiln for a first firing.

Historically, firing and operating the kilns was the most arduous part of the maiolica-making process. Tuscan potteries often had giant, room-sized kilns or *fornaci*, usually constructed of brick and stoked from wood fires beneath the floor. Because of the tremendous resources they required to fire and manage, the kilns were stacked tightly with works and were fired as little as necessary to get the job done. The heat was sometimes regulated by stacking and removing bricks from the doorway to the kiln itself. The works emerged from the kiln with a hard surface and a characteristic terracotta color.

Next, shop assistants dipped each piece into a bath of white, shiny, opaque glaze made from tin oxide to coat the raw terracotta form. Once dry, this tin glaze provided a white background that would form a blank canvas for colored decoration. Glazes made from tin were used in Italy as early as the eleventh century, but became more common as maiolica gained traction in the late 1300s.

After the glaze dried, painters laid colored pigments on the white ground to form designs and scenes. They brought the palette of Tuscany's landscape—deep greens, sapphire blues, gold, and earthen tones—into their designs by obtaining pigments from copper, manganese, iron, antimony, and cobalt. The art of decorating a vessel with these pigments required patience, experience, and above all, a sure hand. There was no going back to correct mistakes, as the pigments immediately bonded with the glaze and were impossible to remove once applied. A second firing in the kiln fused the colors and glaze to the vessel.

As in other ceramic centers of central Italy, the visual vocabulary of the Italian Renaissance breathed life into ceramic wares of Montelupo Fiorentino: scrolls, swags, rosettes, oak leaves, and peacock feather-like patterns populated jars, plates, and other wares. Human figures appeared for the first time in the works of Montelupo Fiorentino around 1400, departing from the centuries-old tradition of vegetal decoration. Idealized nudes, *putti*, and noble people depicted in profile were rendered with the restrained beauty and classical spirit of the Italian Renaissance.

Today, ceramicists in Montelupo source their clay from art supply businesses and use electric kilns to fire their work. In spite of these modern conveniences, the rest of the process of producing maiolica remains more or less the same as it was in centuries past. You can still watch these masters of maiolica preparing vessels and painting them while drawing inspiration from their predecessors some five hundred years ago.

Styles of Montelupo Ceramics

Specialists in Italian ceramics categorize vessels using a staggering number of terms based on period, shape, function, and style. Without turning this section into a compendium, here are some of the most common decorative styles of maiolica you will encounter in Montelupo Fiorentino:

Archaic

Sometimes referred to as proto-maiolica, the term "archaic maiolica" describes the style of ceramics produced in central Italy in the late Middle Ages. You can recognize these wares by the stylized animal and vegetal motifs rendered in a rich blue pigment against a white ground. You will sometimes see these pieces referred to as *a zaffera*, which is a reference to the distinctive cobalt blue used. You will also see them called "Hispano-Moresque," a reference to their stylistic roots in medieval Islamic Spain, with their all-over patterns of stylized leaves, vines, birds, dogs, lions, and other animals. By the fifteenth century, *zaffera a rilievo*, or "relief blue" became popular, using a thick impasto of rich blue that formed a relief pattern across the surface of the vessel.

Damaschino

The "damask" style became popular in the early 1400s, as ceramicists in central Italy began to establish their own visual identity, while still repeating many of the decorative motifs we identify with archaic maiolica. It is unclear whether contemporary observers used the term *damaschino* to refer to the monochromatic blue coloration (pigment of Damascus) or rather to the style, which they may have interpreted as Eastern. The palette remains monochromatic, but the blue is more watercolor-like, a light wash of cobalt over a white background. For the first time, human figures appear in some of these works, but Damaschino is distinguished for its all-over decoration imitating textiles and a more Eastern stylistic vocabulary.

Renaissance

By the end of the fifteenth century, human figures are more common in the works of Montelupo Fiorentino, departing from the centuries-old tradition of vegetal decoration. Sections of decorative elements become more clearly defined, and vegetal elements are more naturalistically rendered. Some ceramicists introduced a distinctive red pigment.

Others began to incorporate a third firing, which resulted in a highly reflective, shiny surface. Lusterware means that a vessel has gone through an additional step after the standard process of maiolica making. After a piece comes out of the kiln from its second firing, it is coated with metallic oxide—usually silver or copper—and undergoes a third firing. This process imparts an iridescent, lustrous finish that became fashionable in Italy in the second half of the fifteenth century.

WHAT KIND OF VESSEL IS IT?

Most ceramic vessels in central Italy fall into well-defined categories based on their function, shapes, and styles. By 1500, a vast typology of ceramic wares had developed in the region. Certain vessels were destined for the table, while others were referred to as *da pompa*, or "for display." Today, ceramics artists draw inspiration from these historical models for more modern wares. Here are some of the most common types you will encounter in Montelupo:

Albarelli and **orciuoli**: Apothecary jars were once commissioned in sets of several hundred for medieval pharmacies and hospitals to contain medicinal herbs and concoctions. An *orciuolo* is typically squatter and occasionally has handles, while an *albarello* tends to be more elongated and sometimes wider at the mouth and base than in the middle. Sometimes these apothecary jars are decorated with text describing their contents (for example, oregano or mustard seed).

Bacile: a shallow basin

Boccale: a large pitcher or jug with a handle

Ciotola: a shallow bowl

Coppe amatorie: These "lovers' cups" were produced as trophy-like vessels to be given as gifts to spouses, fiancés, and lovers. Sometimes made with a foot or handles, this plate-like shape often features a portrait of a beautiful woman—sometimes the recipient of the gift—with a ribbon displaying her name. A *coppa amatoria* was almost always considered *da pompa*, or for display.

Piatto: a plate

Scodella or scodellone: a large, flat-bottomed basin

How to Buy Maiolica

The best advice is not to buy maiolica in Florence at all. Instead, make the short trip to Montelupo Fiorentino, located about twenty kilometers to the west of Florence along the Arno River. The narrow alleys of Montelupo Fiorentino are lined with street signs and house numbers marked by ceramic tiles with bright flourishes of blue. This artistic detail in the urban fabric points to the history of the town as a historical supplier of ceramics to Florence and beyond.

Montelupo is not particularly charming, but it is a great choice for an easy-to-reach destination that boasts a small yet thriving community of traditional ceramicists. The town is far enough off the beaten path enough so that crowds are few and prices are reasonable. In Montelupo, you can meet face to face with maiolica makers, and come away with a better understanding of the technical process, as well as a more immersive travel experience. Buying directly also means getting a much better value. In Florence itself, you will pay top price for maiolica, as well as miss out on the chance to experience meeting these masters firsthand.

Once you've made the trip to Montelupo Fiorentino, it's hard to go wrong as long as you buy directly from the maker, but be careful: the quality is all in the finishing touches. The execution of the painted decoration distinguishes higher-quality work from lesser-quality wares. Some workshops, especially those with larger production, tend to rely on stencils to form the most common decorative motifs used in their work such as rosettes, leaves, and other patterns that are frequently repeated. A freehand drawing that is done with extra time, care, and great skill is often more nuanced, and will result in a more beautiful and richly decorated piece. Some pieces are finished with a combination of freehand and stenciled painting. Take the time to look carefully and compare the quality of the painting before you buy.

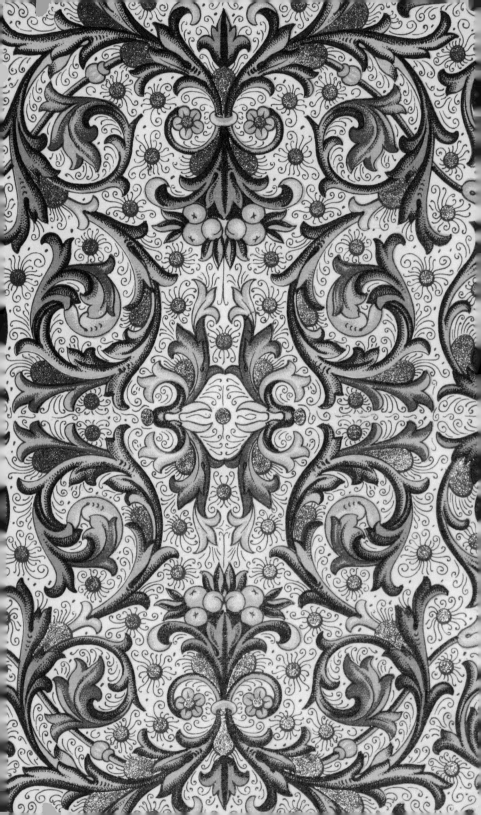

6

Paper & Bookbinding

By the end of the fifteenth century, some eighty paper shops were documented in Florence, a surprisingly large number for a population that numbered only around seventy thousand at that time. In fact, Florence claims an important position in the history of bookmaking and publishing. The city's preeminence in international trade, its concentration of humanist scholars, and its centuries-old artisanal heritage made Florence a natural setting for large-scale bookmaking to take root.

Prior to Johann Gutenberg's invention of moveable type in the 1450s, each and every book was handmade. Parchment vellum was laboriously prepared by treating sheepskins in the tanneries. A parchment sheath was never discarded, only occasionally scraped down and reused in a new book. Books were precious, expensive, and coveted, prized possessions of monasteries and learned collectors wealthy enough to purchase them. A book remained out of reach for the average person, who may not have had the money to purchase one or even the ability to read at all.

Florentine monasteries and other ecclesiastical institutions held extensive libraries and were also deeply involved in the transcription, production, and illustration of precious manuscripts. Florentine noble families such as the Strozzi and the Gaddi prided themselves on their private collections of illuminated manuscripts and other valuable texts, which functioned as much as markers of social status as of scholarship.

Under Cosimo I de Medici, the father of the Medici dynasty, Florence became the epicenter of a thriving bookmaking culture. In the early fifteenth century, Cosimo attracted a group of intellectuals who fostered what would later be known as Renaissance humanism, a new cultural ideal based on the idea of reformulating works of ancient Greece and Rome. The renewed interest

FLORENTINE HUMANISM AND THE ARTS

The intellectual movement known as "Renaissance humanism" affected much more than just the book trade in Florence. Within a single generation, peoples' attitudes about objects and their makers would shift dramatically, such that in 1550, Giorgio Vasari—not incidentally, a Florentine and a friend of Michelangelo—published an influential book called *Lives of the Most Excellent Painters, Sculptors, and Architects*, elevating these types of creators to rockstar status by sharing juicy biographical details.

In the mind of the public, painting, sculpture, and architecture began to be considered "art," and their makers creative masterminds—"artists." Meanwhile those who maintained guild traditions and faithfully produced candlesticks, ceramic vessels, gold jewelry, or wrought-iron gates would be known communally as "artisans," and their works considered "minor" or "decorative arts," connoting an unjustly inferior status and solidifying the distinction between "art" and "craft" that still persists in the Western world.

in studying, transcribing, and interpreting ancient texts propelled Florentine bookmaking to unprecedented heights, as demand for these works increased and new printing techniques allowed these books to be more widely disseminated.

One of the most influential Renaissance humanists was Niccolò de' Niccoli, a scholar and son of a Florentine wool merchant. Niccoli amassed an extraordinary private library of ancient manuscripts that caught the attention of Cosimo I de Medici. Niccoli became a passionate leader in the community of learned humanists under Cosimo's patronage. Niccoli's avid book collecting would be eclipsed only by the Medici themselves. Over the next two generations, the Medici family assembled one of the most famous collections of texts from the ancient world. Cosimo's sons continued their father's tradition of commissioning illuminated manuscripts. By the reign of Cosimo's grandson, Lorenzo the Magnificent, in the late fifteenth century, the Medici library had become an important center of research.

Traditional monastic scriptoria could no longer meet the exploding demand for new books that occurred over the course of the fifteenth century. With the innovations made in moveable type, engraving, book printing, and distribution by the late 1400s, Florence was poised to be a leader in this expanding trade. A community of publishers, printers, and bookbinders was established in Florence by the mid-fifteenth century and these professionals enjoyed esteemed social status. Profiting from merchants traveling centuries-old international trade routes, Florentine printers and publishers found easy distribution channels to the newly emerging booksellers across Europe.

One of the most influential publishers of the era was the Giunti family. The Giunti were already established in the Florentine wool trade when the family sent its youngest son, Lucantonio, to Venice in 1491 to learn about the world of printing. Returning home, the Giunti began to typeset volumes of medical, legal, liturgical, and humanist texts. Their books in Greek, Latin, and vernacular

AN EXTRAORDINARY LIBRARY

The Laurentian Library in Florence was the lucky recipient of many ecclesiastical and private Florentine collections of books. It contains some 3,000 manuscripts from the Medici family alone, a collection the family opened to the public in 1571 in an impressive building designed by Michelangelo. At that time, the Medici books, all bound in matching red leather covers with the family coat of arms, were chained to the benches so that readers could peruse them without slipping out of the library with one of these treasures under their cloaks.

languages were soon destined for intellectuals, universities, and collectors all over Europe. The Giunti sent members of their extended family to set up presses in Rome; in Lyon, France; and in Salamanca, Spain, spreading their influence internationally. Nonetheless, they printed the Florentine fleur-de-lis as a printers' mark at the front of every book they published.

In Florence itself, book production was a natural occupation for artisans who were already skilled at working with leather, pigments, and gold leaf. The production of Florentine books involved specialists of several stripes—masters of leather, paper, engraving, printing, gilding, and other trades.

The earliest book pages were made of parchment, which comes from animal hides, and of course many of the book bindings were made of leather, so it's no surprise that the book and leather industries were closely tied. In fact, at the beginning of the thirteenth century, the Florentine parchment-makers (*pergamenai*) formed part of the same guild as the book binders (*legatori dei libri*). Soon, paper would be added to this arsenal of book-making skills. Paper-making made its way from Asia to Europe during the Middle Ages. Paper may have entered Italy through Venice, with its strategic location as the gateway to the Eastern world. From Venice, the tradition of decorative papers moved south to Florence, where it also flourished.

With the widespread use of moveable type instead of script, paper instead of vellum, and woodblock prints and engravings instead of hand-painted illuminations, the interior pages of books were dramatically transformed from their medieval predecessors. A book's exterior binding, however, remained essentially the same as its medieval models. Often, the *legatoria* only bound a book once a patron purchased it, and therefore the binding was customized and could be as simple or as fancy as the book buyer's budget and desire.

Early bookbinders discovered that when leather bindings came into direct contact with end papers, the result was discoloration and damage to the paper. They began facing the inside of the leather covers with hand-colored papers. This practice not only created blank pages for creative and colorful paper displays, but later the bookbinders also realized they could reduce the amount of expensive leather they used in binding. Eventually, many bookbinders began using leather only for the spine, disguising the cover boards with colorful decorative papers.

The practice of decorating paper with colorful patterns that imitate marble and textiles probably originated in China. By the fifteenth century, these techniques had made their way across East and Central Asia. While the practice of using marbleized end papers was widespread in Germany and France by the seventeenth and eighteenth centuries, most Florentine and other Italian bookbinders used surprisingly little colored decoration, preferring plain, white end papers and focusing on the leather binding of the book itself. By the mid-eighteenth century, several prominent Florentine bookmakers incorporated marbleized and patterned paper into their repertory of woodblock prints, copperplate engraving, leather binding, and other book production services.

Florence also became an important center for engraving during the fifteenth century. The technique of engraving involves using a metal tool called a burin to gouge patterns into a metal plate, coating the plate with ink, then pressing paper onto it in order to transfer the image. Originally, engraving probably derived from goldsmithing and more specifically the technique of niello, so it's no wonder that it caught on as early as the 1400s in Florence. These engravings appeared inside of books, but also decorated the inside of keepsake boxes and other treasured possessions of their Florentine patrons. The works of many famous Florentine painters appear in an enormous number of engravings and etchings, some of which were destined for bound books.

Although the paper and book trade was already well established by the time English visitors began making Florence a required stop on a Grand Tour of Europe in the eighteenth century, it was these "Grand Tourists" who helped bring a new wave of interest in paper and books to Florence. Wealthy English travelers fueled demand for individual prints and books that contained engravings by these highly regarded artists. These artists' *vedute*—or views—of Florence served as precursors to modern-day postcards for these international visitors who wanted to take a piece of Florence home with them. By the end of the 1700s, a flourishing Anglo-Italian community helped keep the book and paper trade alive.

How Books are Made

The first step in traditional bookbinding involves ensuring that all the folios or signatures (gathered sections of a book) are properly ordered and assembled. Traditionally, the text block is then placed into a frame and sewn together with linen thread and long cords of vellum or leather. A modest softbound cover made of parchment, vellum, or leather might be attached by threading the linen threads through the cover and sewing them tight.

More expensive hardcover bindings are achieved by attaching stiff pasteboards to a hinged spine. The laces of the text block are fastened to the edge of the pasteboards. Finally, the pasteboards and spine would be covered with leather, which may be punched, stamped tooled, gilded, or decorated using specialized book-making tools.

Marbleized paper (*carta marmorizzata*) is made by swirling pigments into a large, shallow pan of water, then laying the paper gently and briefly on the surface of the water to transfer the pattern. Because the designs sometimes mimic the natural veining in stone or marble, the word "marbleized" came to be used.

Marbleized paper is made across Asia and Europe, turned out with differing techniques depending on where it is made. In Florence, paper makers traditionally began with viscous oil-based paints well-known to Florentine artists since the late Middle Ages. These pigments, known as *size* or *sizing*, derived from various plants. Today, many paper artists prefer synthetic acrylics

---

FLORENTINE FOLIOS

Florence boasts a handful of excellent antiquarian bookstores, some in business for a century or longer. These *librerie* are wonderful places full of historical atmosphere and unique works of Florentine history. Keep your eye out for hand-bound volumes and printers' marks or logos in the first few pages, which will give you information about the origin of the publisher or printer. And don't forget about prints, many of which were detached from antique books at some point in the past. You can pick up beautiful etchings and engravings by known Florentine artists at bookstores and antique shops across the city.

and oil paints. Artists apply the paints into a wide, shallow tray filled with water. Sometimes a surfactant is used to help the colors float on the surface. Traditionally, artists used ox gall to serve this purpose, though today there are synthetic surfactants on the market.

The creative aspect of paper marbling comes next, when the artist applies the colors to the water using any number of techniques—like dropping or splattering paint using paintbrushes, horsehair or straw whisks, or other tools—to apply color to the surface of the water in a particular design or order. After the color has been dropped, the artist may use a variety of tools—including rakes, styluses, combs, brushes, or even a single hair—to create swirls, lines, and other design elements in the paint.

How to Buy Florentine Books and Paper

Shops all over Florence sell blocks of elegant stationery, sheaths of handmade paper, leather-bound books with decorative end papers, and a host of related items from fountain pens to wax seals, agendas, diaries, and calendars. Most of the books you see in the shops are commercially bound, and the decorative end papers are machine-printed rather than handmade. There are, however, a few old-fashioned *legatorie* fashioning book bindings and making papers by hand. Resist the temptation to scarf up something from the many shops catering to tourists and seek out the artisanal makers instead.

The most cost-efficient and authentic approach to buying paper is to buy handmade pieces by the sheet. These papers may be used as giftwrap or framed and hung on the wall for a beautiful display. Packaged into a stiff, cardboard tube, handmade paper sheets make an ideal portable Florentine souvenir. Finally, if you are interested in pursuing bookbinding, engraving, or paper making further, you can arrange for a one-on-one or small group class among the city's artisanal bookmakers.

7

Silk & Textiles

The piles of silk ties and scarves that fill the shop windows of Florence are vestiges of a thriving historical trade in silk, wool, and other textiles. In fact, Florence was already established as a textile town as early as the eleventh century, and by the 1300s, trade in cloth was a major part of the Florentine economy. Its merchants made a mint by doing business throughout the rest of Europe. Though the industry declined from the seventeenth century onward, this long history of textile trading formed the basis for the city's preeminence in the world of modern fashion.

Originally, wool rather than silk powered the Florentine economy. According to the Florentine chronicler Giovanni Villani, his native city counted some thirty thousand people involved in the wool trade in 1338. If accurate, that would mean that a full one-third of the population of Florence was involved in some form or another with the production of wool! At that time, the *Arte della Lana*, the guild that governed all aspects of wool production and distribution, wielded inordinate political and cultural influence in the city.

Interestingly, Florentines made their fortunes in wool from sources located outside the city. All of the raw materials came into Florence from elsewhere, and much of the finished product was then re-exported for sale. Their high-quality processes of finishing and dying the wool—in other words, their artisanship—brought Florentines fame, while the business of selling these finished works abroad, even in the face of stiff competition from England and Flanders, brought them fortune.

Bales of wool arrived in the city via muleback from the Tuscan countryside, and later from England and Spain, where sheep were

raised and shorn. The wool then went through twenty-five to thirty steps, from washing and drying, to stretching, combing, spinning, weaving, and dyeing. The entire process was recorded in a fifteenth-century treatise, the *Trattato dell'Arte della Lana*, now preserved in the Riccardiana Library in Florence. Many of these wool-preparing activities were farmed out to independent workers in homes, workshops, commercial offices, and even outdoors. As weaving was traditionally a women's art, many Florentine women made a living spinning and weaving wool in their homes. Many of the dyers or *tintori*, as well as the *tiratoi* (those who stretched the wool), were spread along the Arno, where the flowing river waters facilitated their work. This complex industry faced challenges in the fourteenth century, including the Black Death of the 1340s, which reduced the population of Florence by two-thirds. A revolt of the *ciompi*, or wool carders, also threatened the autonomy and organization of the guilds.

Ultimately, though, the wool industry was eclipsed by another textile tradition with a more enduring connection to the city: silk. At the dawn of the Renaissance, silk represented only a quarter of the size of the wool industry in terms of the number of people working in the sector. Silk shops were located along the via Vaccchereccia, Por Santa Maria, and via Porta Rossa, just off the Piazza della Signoria.

Although silk had been imported to Florence throughout the Middle Ages and traded far and wide by Florentine merchants, it began to be dyed and finished in the city toward the end of the Middle Ages. A fiscal census of 1404 lists some one hundred silk weavers in the city at that time, and silk grew in importance over the course of the 1400s. Prior to this time, goldsmiths had been involved in the making of gold and silver thread to be used in textiles, but by the 1420s the silk makers were taking this on themselves. The silk guild, or the *Arte della Seta*, incorporated both silk merchants as well as producers, and silk emerged as an important part of the artisanal fabric of Florence from then on.

THE FLORENTINE FABRIC

Silk and other textiles were closely related to the leather trade, as they were all used to produce apparel. In addition, the same sheep hide might supply a maker of leather armor as well as a weaver. The complex Florentine guild system, or the *arti*, tightly regulated makers of everything from shoes, belts, purses, embroidery, hosiery, satin, taffeta, brocade, damask, velvet, and jewelry. Guild statutes controlled the production of these items and strict sumptuary laws stipulated the wearing of apparel made with them.

Sweeping sumptuary laws recorded in the fourteenth century stipulated exactly how Florentine citizens could dress in public to ensure appropriate behavior and avoid sinfully extravagant displays. They specified limits on certain types of clothing and jewelry, down to the types fabrics and even dye quality. To our modern eyes, these laws are fascinating to the point of being unbelievable. A sixteenth-century Florentine diary captures how these sumptuary laws affected how Florentine men dressed during the workday, governing the use of a traditional long woolen tunic known as a *lucco*:

As Florence is founded on the guilds and on mercantile traffic, citizens can more easily look after their business, shops, and trade and lead a healthy life and move around if they wear a black cloak and apron, which comes down just below the knee. This they can wear during their workdays in the morning until the bell of the Uffizi. But after the bell they must wear the *lucco* until they go back home for lunch. After the

**noon bell and until the evening bell of the Ave Maria
in winter they must wear the *lucco*.**

On the opposite end of the spectrum, Florentine aristo-
crats might possess so many pieces of luxury clothing that it was
included in their dowries. A 1502 inventory of Lucrezia Borgia's
wardrobe, recorded upon her engagement to Alfonso I of Ferrara,
included some eighty-four gowns, twenty-two headdresses,
eighty-three pairs of shoes or slippers, not to mention jewelry
cases containing some three hundred gemstones and nearly two
thousand pearls!

The Florentine textile industries declined over the course of
the seventeenth and eighteenth centuries, along with those in the
rest of Italy. By the middle of the nineteenth century, however,
several important family artisanal businesses changed the tide
and by the early twentieth century, the modern fashion industry
had begun to take root. Florence, with its centuries-old history
in the textile trade, was poised to play an important role. Guccio
Gucci set up shop in Florence in 1921, producing leather luggage
and handbags to rival those he had seen during a stint as an
immigrant worker at luxury hotels in London and Paris. Salvatore
Ferragamo set up a modest shoe shop in Florence in 1927 that
soon began catering to international celebrities.

In the early 1950s, when Italian fashion pioneer Giovanni
Battista Giorgini began to organize international fashion shows
in the Pitti Palace, these artisanal enterprises were poised to
showcase their goods to the world. Soon, Florence, along with
Milan, began to compete with Paris as one of the world's fashion
capitals. The concept of "Made in Italy" brought film stars,
royalty, and other high-profile buyers to Florence, and they in
turn propelled these once-humble Florentine fashion families
to international fame by projecting an air of exclusivity and
luxury that persists today.

Today, Florence is still home to these venerable fashion
powerhouses, as well as to newer ones like Emilio Pucci, Enrico

Coveri, Roberto Cavalli, and Patrizia Pepe, many centered around the via Tornabuoni and the via della Vigna Nuova. In addition to these famous names, however, Florence boasts dozens of unsung heroes carrying on the tradition of handmade hats, shoes, bags, suits, dresses, and other clothing and accessories.

How Silk is Made

Silk making traces its roots to prehistoric China. For many centuries, the Chinese held a monopoly on sericulture, and silk became famous across the East for its beauty and quality. Eventually, the secrets of silk-making began to leak out as travelers and traders sought to learn about the luxurious material. The Silk Road—a well-trodden system of ancient trade

routes—eventually brought silk to Westerners hungry for these exotic luxuries. By the Middle Ages, Florentine merchants found themselves well positioned to take advantage of this international demand for silk.

Incongruously, this deluxe fabric begins with a worm, or more accurately, a caterpillar. The process starts with the careful cultivation of silkworms, species *Bombyx mori*, along with the mulberry bushes and trees that serve as their habitat and diet. Sericulturists spread the sillkworms and fresh mulberry leaves on large trays stacked in special houses. There the silkworms feast on the leaves and produce a protein filament tightly wound into cocoons. Once completed, the cocoons are sorted and momentarily steamed, which kills the chrysalis, then boiled, which helps loosen the cocoon's delicate filaments. Then, the filaments are "thrown," a process in which several strands are twisted together to yield a thicker, stronger thread. The threads can then be dyed, making them ready to be woven or used in embroidery.

Initially, the Florentines imported the silkworm eggs, cocoons, and mulberry leaves from the East, using their well-connected international trade networks. As the silk industry grew toward the end of the fourteenth century, however, mulberry trees began to be cultivated across Tuscany, so the raw materials for silk making could be sourced in their own backyards. Some of the initial steps of the silk-making process—tending and reeling the cocoons, and spinning thread—were undertaken in silk workers' homes. Weavers operated large wooden handlooms to produce bolts of silk and the dyeing took place in a process similar to that of wool. A central office organized the workers and commercialized the products. In Florence itself, silk production was destined both for apparel and accessories, as well as for textiles used in the home.

How to Buy Silk in Florence

Florence is a world fashion capital and it's impossible to ignore the sparkling flagship stores of some of Italy's most famous luxury brands. Closely associated with Florence, silk neckties and scarves are the bread and butter of many of these world-renowned designers. In addition, smaller Florentine boutiques do a brisk trade in silk accessories. Silk ties and scarves are durable, portable, and, if you know what you're looking at, can be a good value for a high-quality Florentine souvenir.

Keep in mind, however, that the majority of silk ties and scarves in Florence are produced behind the scenes—perhaps in Florence or Tuscany, or perhaps in a factory far distant from the slick boutiques where they are sold. Therefore, it pays to be an educated consumer when it comes to shopping for these sought-after souvenirs, as you will not likely come face-to-face with the person who made them.

A number of synthetic fabrics can masquerade as silk, including acetate, nylon, and polyester. A scarf or tie may be composed entirely of synthetics, or may be made with a silk-synthetic blend. Be sure to examine scarves and ties carefully before buying. Here's what to look for:

Sheen

Genuine silk is famous for its beautiful shine. As you turn the scarf or tie over in your hand in raking light, you should be able to see different colors shine through, the result of differently colored threads used in the warp and weft.

Texture

Pure silk feels exceptionally smooth and slippery in your hands. When you rub the material vigorously between your hands, do you feel it begin to heat up? If so, it's a good sign of authentic silk.

Weave

Most scarves and ties are machine-woven, which makes genuine silk difficult to distinguish from synthetics, because the stitching of both appear perfect to the eye. Hand-woven silk, more common in upholstery and home textiles, incorporates small imperfections, or slubs, in the weave.

Stitching

Check the stitching on the back of the tie or along the sides of the scarf. Artisanal ties will be more thickly woven, hand-folded, and hand-stitched. A high-quality scarf will have edges that have been rolled and stitched by hand in a thread that blends with the colors along the edges of the design.

Pattern

On silk, a design may be woven or printed. Many textiles for the home, such as decorative pillowcases and upholstery, are woven, sometimes on a traditional handloom. In this case, you will see the pattern on both sides, with the underside distinguished by its slightly fuzzy appearance. In contrast, most scarves are printed using a silkscreen process using modern printing machines. The highest-quality scarves will be printed using a traditional, time-consuming process that involves pulling a different-colored screen across a metal frame by hand, building the design one color at a time.

Sound

If you rub pure silk between your fingers, it makes a distinctive crunching sound that is often described as similar to walking on freshly fallen snow.

Price

If the price is too good to be true, it isn't real silk. Genuine silk is relatively expensive compared to synthetic imitations, often several times more.

If you're still not sure, you can perform the "ring test." Unless it's exceptionally large or thickly woven, you can remove your wedding band or other ring and pull a silk scarf right through it. The scarf should glide through smoothly with no resistance. Synthetic fabrics tend to bunch or tug, making it difficult to pass them through a ring.

The definitive test of genuine silk, though, is the "burn test." If you set the fringe or a thread of a silk scarf ablaze with a match or a lighter, you will hear it singe, then see it disintegrate into a tiny smoldering pile of fine ash, releasing an aroma akin to burnt

SCARFING UP AN AUTHENTIC SOUVENIR

Sadly, foreign-made knockoffs populate many of the boutiques selling scarves across Florence. The traditional Florentine scarf is a square, with edges that have been rolled and stitched by hand. Most merchants will allow you to open and spread out a scarf to check the pattern, weave, and stitching, as well as the quality of the silk, so take the time to examine it carefully.

hair. The burn test quickly unmasks plastic-smelling synthetic threads that curl or melt when burned. A silk merchant might be willing to perform this test for you, but I don't recommend doing it in a store yourself!

Amidst the sparkle and flash of Florentine fashion, authentic textile artisans such as artisanal tailors, upholsterers, and silk weavers remain unjustly overlooked. If you have your heart set on a sartorial souvenir, Florentine tailors are world-renowned for turning your dreams into reality, so take advantage of the opportunity to have a shirt, dress, hat, or suit custom made for you. Some Florentine tailors possess exceptional skill and experience in turning the fabric of your choice into a piece of apparel that is one of a kind.

While fashion apparel stands at the top of the shopping list for many visitors to Florence, don't overlook upholstery fabrics, tapestry, drapery, pillow covers, bedding, and other textiles used in the home. Herein lies the opportunity to experience the centuries-old tradition of Florentine silk and wool firsthand. In fact, several Florentine textile enterprises boast pedigrees that reach back to the 1600s. Some even use generations-old handlooms to create breathtakingly beautiful fabrics whose quality is truly among the world's finest. Best of all, you can watch it being made.

Resources

Visiting Florentine Artisans

M any stores and artisan workshops in Florence are multi-generational enterprises, some in operation for a century or even longer. However, change is inevitable and sooner or later, businesses relocate or close. The older members of the family pass on, and the new generation takes the family traditions in a new direction. It is frustrating for travelers to go to the trouble to buy a guidebook and locate an artisan studio, only to find it shuttered or relocated. For this reason, rather than listing specific artisans here, I have created a separate ebook complement to this guide called *Artisans of Florence*. You can download the book directly to your computer or ereader free of charge by following the instructions at the front or back of this book. I conceived *Artisans of Florence* as a digital complement to this book, which is published in both digital and print editions. My goal for *Artisans of Florence* is to keep the artisan listings as up-to-date as possible in order to ensure the best experience for you as a traveler and shopper.

While having a list of high-quality artisans is convenient, it does not replace the abilities of a discerning shopper. The skills you need to select a quality piece of ceramics or a high-quality gold ring will never change. It's all about training your eye to recognize styles, patterns, artistic conventions, quality, tradition, and value. With this book, *Authentic Arts: Florence*, it is my goal to arm you with the information you need to make smart choices, no matter which shop or market you visit. The resources below should put you well on your way to being among the most informed, educated shopper in Florence. Enjoy your trip!

Museum Collections of Authentic Florentine Arts

The Galleria dell'Accademia and the Uffizi Gallery stand among the world's most important art museums and are must-sees in spite of the crowds. Outside of these two institutions, however, stand an impressive number of lesser-known museums around Florence. These fantastic collections are a treasure trove of authentic arts and they are also a great place to train your eye before you visit artisan studios and shops. Before you buy anything, spend some time looking at historical examples of the works you have in mind. You'll come away with the ability to recognize traditional colors, patterns, styles, and conventions, and you'll be better equipped to discern quality and authenticity when you hit the streets. Check the museum web sites for current information about opening hours and admission fees, and to buy tickets online where available.

FLORENCE

Bardini Museum

Museo Stefano Bardini

Via dei Renai, 37

055/2342427

http://museicivicifiorentini.comune.fi.it/en/bardini/

The Bardini Museum displays the private collection of the art dealer Stefano Bardini, who died in 1922 and donated his collection to the city of Florence. The museum is housed in a former convent that was renovated and repurposed as a Florentine palazzo by Bardini himself in the 1880s. In addition to an impressive collection of medieval and Renaissance sculpture and panel painting, the museum also includes a series of beautiful wooden dowry chests, arms and armor, works of maiolica, and gilded picture frames. The museum also contains the original bronze statue of the *porcellino*, the famous boar whose replica is now one of the main tourist attractions in the Mercato Nuovo. If you've ever rubbed the boar's nose in hope of returning to Florence one day, you know the one!

Bargello Museum

Museo Nazionale del Bargello

Via del Proconsolo, 4

055/2388606

www.polomuseale.firenze.it

museobargello@polomuseale.firenze.it

In addition to its large and celebrated collection of medieval and Renaissance sculpture, the Bargello also holds a lesser-known assortment of maiolica ceramics, textiles, and other works of Florentine history. Of special note are the breathtakingly beautiful objects in bronze, silver, and gold, including an impressive collection of Florentine armor and parade helmets.

Costume Gallery

Galleria del Costume
Palazzina della Meridiana
Pitti Palace
055/2388611
www.polomuseale.firenze.it

The Galleria del Costume traces the history of fashion with a rotating display of some six thousand works ranging from the sixteenth to the twentieth centuries, including clothing, theater costumes, and pieces worn by famous stars of stage and screen. The museum includes works by some of Italy's most famous fashion houses, including Armani, Missoni, Valentino, Versace, and others. One of the highlights is the restored gown of Eleonora of Toledo, the wife of Cosimo I de Medici; Bronzino's portrait of Eleonora wearing that dress is across the Arno in the Uffizi Gallery. A museum ticket to the Costume Gallery will also gain you entrance to the Silver Museum and the Porcelain Museum, located in the same palace complex.

Contini Bonacossi Collection

Uffizi Gallery
Entrance on the via Lambertesca (back side of the Uffizi Gallery)
055/2388809
www.uffizi.firenze.it

The Uffizi Gallery acquired the Contini Bonacossi Collection, an outstanding private holding that includes eleven large coats of arms made in maiolica by the fifteenth-century della Robbia workshop. Other masterpieces include furniture, paintings, and sculpture of the Renaissance. The Contini Bonacossi Collection is located in a separate building from the Uffizi Gallery and has a separate entrance and hours. Check ahead of time for its opening schedule as it varies according to the time of year and fluctuations in staff. If you're lucky enough to work this collection into your travel itinerary, you will have witnessed one of the city's hidden gems!

Ferragamo Museum

Museo Salvatore Ferragamo

Palazzo Spini Feroni

Piazza Santa Trinita, 5r

055/3562846

www.ferragamo.com/museo

museoferragamo@ferragamo.com

Shoe fanatics: You know who you are! The Ferragamo family opened this museum, offering the public a fascinating insight into the history of shoemaking. The collection, on the lower level of the company's original headquarters, includes shoes, of course, but also thousands of wooden lasts, shoe models, sketches, magazines, and other paraphernalia from Salvatore Ferragamo's prolific creative decades between the late 1920s and the 1960s.

Foundation for Florence Artisans

Fondazione Firenze Artigianato Artistico

Vecchio Conventino, Spazio Arti e Mestieri

Via Giano della Bella, 20/1

055/2322269

www.fondazioneartigianato.it

info@fondazioneartigianato.it

Many travelers don't realize that the artisan shops you see on the streets represent a small fraction of the overall artisan population in Florence. Many Florentine artisans work from studios in their homes, or scattered elsewhere without a retail presence. Now, this relatively new foundation has set up a wonderful space for visitors to watch traditional craftspeople demonstrate what they do best. The workspaces are organized inside an old convent a stone's throw from the Boboli Gardens and the Pitti Palace. Here you can watch masters practicing mosaic, woodturning, metalworking, painting, restoration, leather, glass, and other pursuits, all under one roof. Best of all, you can talk directly with them about their work.

Gucci Museum

Gucci Museo
Piazza della Signoria, 10
055/75923302
www.guccimuseo.com
guccimuseo@it.gucci.com

The Gucci Museum spans three floors of one of the most historic pieces of real estate in Florence: the fourteenth-century Palazzo della Mercanzia. The palace was originally the center of the city's guilds associated with the manufacture and trade of leather, wool, silk, and other textiles. Essentially the seat of Florence's international commercial power, it is also deeply entwined with the city's artisanal history. Gucci undertook a massive renovation of the building, and today it houses the company's archives and a display of some of its most iconic fashion accessories.

Horne Museum

Museo Horne
Via dei Benci, 6
055/244661
www.museohorne.it
info@museohorne.it

English architect and collector Herbert P. Horne purchased this palazzo in 1911 to house his personal collection of works from the fifteenth and sixteenth centuries. Upon Horne's death, the collection went to the Italian state. Today you can marvel at this eccentric assortment of some of Florence's best artisanal traditions: silver, gold, leather boxes, furniture, textiles, and ceramics. Even better, the museum is rarely crowded so you can get a respite from the crowds and enjoy these beautiful objects up close.

Hospital of the Innocents

Ospedale degli Innocenti
Piazza della Santissima Annunziata, 12
055/2037308
www.istitutodeglinnocenti.it
museo@istitutodeglinnocenti.it

Funded by the wealthy Silk Guild, or *Arte della Seta*, this orphanage building was begun by Filippo Brunelleschi, the same architect responsible for the dome of Florence Cathedral, in 1419. In the spandrels along the exterior arcades, look for the swaddled babies depicted in glazed maiolica roundels. They were designed by the renowned fifteenth-century Florentine ceramic master Andrea della Robbia.

Laurentian Library

Biblioteca Medicea Laurenziana
Piazza San Lorenzo, 9
055/2937911
http://www.bml.firenze.sbn.it
b-mela@beniculturali.it

In 1524, Pope Clement VII—also known as Giulio de Medici, nephew of Lorenzo the Magnificent—commissioned Michelangelo to design a library at San Lorenzo to house the Medici family book collection. The library opened to the public in 1571 and the family's precious volumes, all bound in red leather with the Medici coat of arms, were available for the people to read. Each book was attached to a wooden bench with a chain to avoid theft. Today you can still appreciate the beauty of Michelangelo's design and see some historic books on rotating display.

Leather School

Scuola del Cuoio

Piazza Santa Croce, 16

055/244533

http://www.scuoladelcuoio.com

info@scuoladelcuoio.com

The leather school began as a collaboration between the monks of Santa Croce and the Gori leather-making family after World War II, with the mission of providing a marketable trade for young people. Today the school caters mostly to international tourists. A photo collection of famous visitors includes everyone from Princess Diana to the golfer Jack Nicklaus. The shop sells purses, wallets, desk accessories, as well as a limited collection of apparel, but the main attraction is the opportunity to watch leather workers at work. If the experience sparks your own creativity, sign up for a course, anywhere from a half-day to nine months. To visit the workshops, buy a ticket for the beautiful church of Santa Croce and include the leather school in your visit, or access the shop directly from its entrance at via San Giuseppe, 5r.

Museum of Inlaid Stone

Opificio delle Pietre Dure

Via Alfani, 78, 055/26511

Viale F. Strozzi, 1 (Fortezza da Basso), 055/46254

www.opificiodellepietredure.it

opd@beniculturali.it

Inlaid stone was the passion of Grand Duke Ferdinand de Medici, who founded and endowed a workshop for this craft in 1588. This highly specialized technique involves inlaying colored semiprecious stones valued for their brilliance and saturated color into furniture and other artwork. The technique is sometimes referred to as intarsia, *commesso* or *opera di commessi*, and is closely allied to mosaic. Today, this specialized, painstaking art of inlaying semiprecious materials like ebony, malachite, ivory, and other stones remains in the hands of a few Florentine artisans. The small Museum of Inlaid Stone is a great place to feast your eyes on a vast array of decorated tabletops, plaques, and other works inlaid with intricate designs that can only be called "painting with stone." The Italian Ministry for Cultural Goods now runs this museum and maintains an important library and conservation center for this art at the Fortezza da Basso.

Palazzo Davanzati House Museum

Via Porta Rossa, 13
055/2388610
www.polomuseale.firenze.it
museo.davanzati@polomuseale.firenze.it

This little-known medieval house museum holds a wonderful collection of Florentine furniture, ceramics, textiles, and other works from the fourteenth to the nineteenth centuries. In the fourteenth century the house belonged to the Davizzi family, who made their fortune as merchants and bankers, and it later passed into the hands of the Davanzati and other families. The antiquarian Elia Volpi restored the building in the nineteenth century and began to share his collection of Florentine antiques in this evocative space.

Pharmacy of Santa Maria Novella

Officina Profumo Farmaceutica di Santa Maria Novella
Via della Scala, 16
055/216276
www.smnovella.it
officina@smnovella.com

One of the oldest continually operating shops in the world, the Officina Profumo Farmaceutica di Santa Maria Novella, founded in 1221, is a marvel and a must-see. The Dominicans, like most monks and nuns across medieval Europe, concocted remedies of medicinal herbs and plants in their pharmacy. They stored these salves, medicines, and balms in jars made of maiolica ceramics and treated the sick in the monastic infirmary. In 1612, the Dominicans opened their pharmacy to the Florentine public, selling perfumes and medicines. Their skill at concocting pharmaceutical products soon brought them worldwide fame. The museum displays antique pharmacy jars and equipment used to prepare medicinal herbs and treat patients. Today, the shop is worth a trip just for its beautiful interior, but you might want to try out their famous rose water, floral extracts, or almond paste lotions.

Silver Museum

Museo degli Argenti

Piazza Pitti, 1

055/2388709

www.polomuseale.firenze.it

argenti@polomuseale.firenze.it

The main attraction of this museum is the incredible "Medici treasure" on display. It is impossible to convey in words the intricacy, opulence, and technical mastery of metalworking represented by this fascinating private collection of the Medici family. The large holding of vases, implements, tableware, and ceremonial objects made of bronze, gold, silver, semiprecious stones, cameos, and rock crystal is staggering, a feast for the eyes. The museum entrance is on the left-hand side of the imposing façade of the Pitti Palace, once the summer ground-floor apartments of the Medici. Check out the porcelain and costume collections while you're there.

NEAR FLORENCE

BORGO SAN LORENZO

Chini Museum

Museo Chini
Villa Pecori Giraldi
Borgo San Lorenze / Mugello (FI)
055/8456230
www.museochini.it
museo@museochini.it

If you are a fan of Art Nouveau—referred to sometimes in Italy as Liberty Style—you will enjoy a trip to the Chini Museum located in Borgo San Lorenzo, about twenty kilometers northeast of Florence. At the turn of the twentieth century, the artist Galileo Chini founded a ceramics center called Arte della Ceramica. He brought together a group of Tuscan maiolica specialists to ply their skills in the interest of the new style, popular in Europe, based on vegetal forms and overall decorative schemes that incorporated architecture, furniture, and interior decoration. Chini won many international prizes for his works in ceramic and other media. Today, the museum, located inside the picturesque Villa Pecori Giraldi, traces the history of the Chini production as well as Art Nouveau in Italy.

MONTELUPO FIORENTINO

Ceramics Museum
Museo Archeologico e della Ceramica
Palazzo del Podestà
Piazza Vittorio Veneto 10/11
Montelupo Fiorentino (FI)
0571/51352
www.museomontelupo.it

When most people think of Italian ceramics, they think of maiolica—the rich, colorful wares that became famous in the fourteenth, fifteenth, and sixteenth centuries in major ceramics centers across the Italian peninsula. While Florentines consumed maiolica ceramics in great volume, the fear of fire breaking out was so great that most ceramics were imported from towns outside of the city. Ceramicists in Montelupo Fiorentino supplied the Florentine demand for maiolica, but their works were also exported as far as London and Constantinople. With more than five thousand pieces dating from the thirteenth century onward, you can trace the history of this important Tuscan ceramics tradition in the museum displays. After your visit to the museum, shop among the wonderful artists still at work in this ceramics capital just twenty kilometers west of Florence along the Arno.

SESTO FIORENTINO

Doccia / Richard-Ginori Museum
Museo di Doccia / Richard-Ginori
Viale Pratese, 31
Sesto Fiorentino (FI)
055/4207767
www.richardginori1735.com
museo@richardginori1735.com

The Marchese Carlo Ginori founded a porcelain manufacture in Doccia, on the western outskirts of Florence, in 1735 and enjoyed a monopoly on porcelain production in Tuscany for decades. In 1896, the Milanese firm Società Ceramica Richard incorporated the Ginori porcelain works and the company became known as Richard-Ginori. Richard-Ginori

declared bankruptcy in January 2013 and was purchased by Gucci. It will be interesting to see what the luxury powerhouse does with this old porcelain works. For now, call ahead to make sure the Doccia Museum is open before making an excursion to Sesto Fiorentino.

Festivals & Events

Italians take their festivals seriously and in Florence, the variety and frequency of its traditional festivals means that there is something authentic to experience all year round. Nearly anything can be cause for celebration—saints' days, religious or civic holidays, and remembrances of important historical events all warrant festivals. Traditional arts often take center stage at these cultural extravaganzas, as they serve as a source of local pride and collective memory. Here are Florentine festivals in which artisanal traditions play a key role:

MONTHLY

Antiques and Artisans Market
Santo Spirito Market
Second Sunday of the month

A few dozen Florentine artisans cluster in the piazza Santo Spirito for a craft and antiques market on the second Sunday of each month. You may hear locals refer to this market as *arti e mestieri* (arts and trades), and you can find everything from junk to fine art, food, furniture, and sometimes a truly surprising find.

Antiques Market
Piazza Ciompi Market
Last Sunday of the Month

If you are a fan of flea markets and rummage sales, you will enjoy browsing the Piazza Ciompi Monday through Saturday, as junk sellers run stalls full of small curiosities from postcards to coins to mismatched tableware. On the last Sunday of the month the market expands, overflowing with vintage furniture, books, jewelry, clothing, and other finds. Keep your eyes out for gently used Florentine artisanal treasures like leather bags and jackets or antique pieces of silver or jewelry.

Antiques Market
Fortezza Antiquaria
Third weekend of the month

The imposing Fortezza da Basso forms the backdrop of this monthly antiques and flea market, usually open from about 9:00am until dusk.

JANUARY

Cavalcade of the Magi

Cavalcata dei Magi

January 6

Epiphany, a national holiday in Italy celebrated on January 6, is equivalent to the twelfth day of Christmas and commemorates the visit of the three kings bearing gifts to the Christ Child. In Italy, however, the religious significance of this holiday is typically overshadowed by the arrival of Befana, a witch-like, broom-riding old woman who, according to tradition, leaves candy in children's stockings the night before Epiphany. The Florentine cavalcade was renewed in the 1990s, but is based on a celebration documented as early as 1417, in which the males of the Medici family took part. The procession through the streets is a fun opportunity to glimpse sumptuous Renaissance costumes.

MARCH

Florentine New Year

Capodanno Fiorentino

Sunday following March 25

Europeans used to celebrate the New Year on March 25, the Feast of the Annunciation, marking nine months before the birth of Christ. There is a procession from the Palagio di Parte Guelfa to the Basilica di Santissima Annunziata, with Florentines in traditional costume.

MARCH-APRIL

Artisan Exhibition
Mostra Mercato Internazionale dell'Artigianato
Last week of April
http://www.mostraartigianato.it

One of the Italian craft industry's most important trade shows overtakes the historic Fortezza da Basso each year, with an emphasis on the trades of Tuscany—leather, wrought iron, gilded woodwork, antiques, painting, and more. The works of a few other countries are also represented.

Antiques Market
Mostra-mercato dell'antiquariato
Montelupo Fiorentino (outside of Florence)
www.comune.montelupo-fiorentino.fi.it

This semi-annual antiques market usually takes place in the Piazza dell'Unione Europea and assembles an interesting jumble of furniture and antiques. Among the goods, occasionally a work of ceramic appears. If you find a quality piece of ceramics from Montelupo, you've found a treasure! Check the town's web site for updated event dates and information.

"Explosion of the Cart"
Scoppio del Carro
Easter Sunday

This annual spectacle is a local favorite. It centers around a street parade and fireworks display set off from an elaborately carved wooden wagon dating from 1622. Once it arrives in the Piazza del Duomo, a dove-shaped rocket symbolizing the Holy Spirit sets off a big bang and the fireworks follow.

JUNE

International Ceramics Festival

Festa internazionale della ceramica

Third week

Montelupo Fiorentino

www.festaceramica.it

Normally a quiet town, Montelupo Fiorentino pulls out all the stops at its annual celebration of ceramics. The festival offers an opportunity to meet face to face with many of Montelupo Fiorentino's contemporary ceramics artists, some of whose workshops are not typically accessible other times of year. Around town, ceramics exhibitions and live demonstrations take place over several days. Local food, children's activities, live music, and other special events make it a destination for many Tuscans and visitors from further afield.

Feast of St. John the Baptist & Historic Football Game

Calcio Storico

June 24

June 24 marks the feast of John the Baptist, the patron saint of Florence, and includes a parade of colorful Renaissance costumes. An historic football match—a peculiarly Florentine combination of soccer, rugby, and wrestling—takes place in the Piazza Santa Croce. This rowdy game pits four Florentine neighborhoods against one another, with different colors for team members from Santa Croce, Santo Spirito, Santa Maria Novella, and San Giovanni. What makes this game even more interesting is that the players wear those Renaissance costumes while roughhousing one another for the privilege of taking home a prized cow as a trophy.

OCTOBER

Antiques Market

Mostra-mercato dell'antiquariato

Montelupo Fiorentino (outside of Florence)

www.comune.montelupo-fiorentino.fi.it

This semi-annual antiques market is the same as the one that takes place in April (see above).

Ceramics Fair

Fiera della Ceramica

First weekend in October

Organized by the Arte della Ceramica in the Piazza Santissima Annunziata, this relatively new ceramics fair tends to focus on contemporary ceramic arts rather than the traditional maiolica of Tuscany, but it's worth a trip if it fits into your Florence travels.

DECEMBER

Artisan Exhibition

Mostra Mercato Internazionale dell'Artigianato

Rotating dates

http://www.mostraartigianato.it

This event is primarily geared toward the gift trade and is a smaller version of the International Craft Exhibition that takes place in April (see above). The focus is on holiday crafts, such as nativity figures, Christmas ornaments and decoration, and toys.

Other Surprising Discoveries

Museums and artisan studios are not the only places in Florence to explore traditional arts. Some of the most fascinating and authentic finds appear in unexpected places—in a little-known chapel, in a street-corner shrine, on a sign in the alleyway. Don't miss these fun opportunities to immerse yourself in Florentine artisanal history.

A MIND-BOGGLING DISPLAY OF INLAID STONE

Princes' Chapel

Cappella dei Principi

Museo delle Cappelle Medicee

Piazza di Madonna degli Aldobrandini, 6

055/2388602

www.polomuseale.firenze.it

The so-called Princes' Chapel or Cappella dei Principi is an octagonal, domed chapel within the complex of the Basilica of San Lorenzo. It was designed in the early 1600s as the final resting place of the Medici rulers. What distinguishes this Renaissance chapel from all the others in Florence is the incredible display of *commessi*, or inlaid stonework composed of semiprecious stones, that cover every inch of the chapel interior. The stones are sawn and assembled into designs or paintings with pieces fitted together like a complex jigsaw puzzle. The large-scale stone works known as the Opificio delle Pietre Dure was established to produce the work specifically for this chapel. The effect is overwhelming, a multicolored mass of stonework that covers every inch of space in the chapel, the revetments entirely covered by complex design. A ticket to this museum encompasses the Cappella dei Principi, the crypt, the treasury of the Basilica of San Lorenzo, as well as a sacristy designed by Michelangelo.

ARTISANAL COATS OF ARMS

Tribunal Palace

Tribunale della Mercanzia

Piazza della Signoria

When disputes inevitably arose between Florentine merchants, they were adjudicated in a civic tribunal specifically designed to carry out litigation related to business. Fittingly, the building, dating back to the 1350s, is decorated with the coats of arms of some of the city's most powerful guilds or *arti*. Most travelers miss this interesting detail, so don't cross the busy Piazza della Signoria without looking up to take

note of the sculpted shields with each guild's emblem. Gucci has completed a massive restoration of this building, and now houses its company museum inside it.

EVEN MORE COATS OF ARMS

Tabernacle with coats of arms

Orsanmichele

Via Calzaiuoli

At the end of the fourteenth century, this former grain market was converted into the chapel of the city's powerful trade guilds. Each guild commissioned a statue of its patron saint to decorate the façade and the coats of arms of each guild are displayed on a great tabernacle inside the church.

Street Signs that Recall
Traditional Trades of Florence

Centuries ago, many artisans operated retail shops on the street level of their homes and lived in rooms on the upper stories. These ground-level shops often had a counter or window so people could transact business on the street.

One of my favorite things to do in Florence is to "read" its history as I walk. Whether you read Italian or just have a good dictionary, pay attention to the street signs. The great rectangular etched stones tell the story of the city. What's more, the makers of shoes, silk, leather, and other centuries-old trades live on through these markers of their memory. Here are some streets that retain the memory of their old trades:

Brickyard: Via della Mattonaia

Buckle makers: via dei Fibbiai

Ceramic kilns: via delle Fornaci

Dyers: Via dei Tintori and Corso dei Tintori

Shoemakers: Via dei Calzauoli

Skinners (associated with the tanners and furriers): via Pellicceria

Stretching grounds for wool production: piazza del Tiratoio

Tanners: via dei Conciatori

Keep your eyes out for these and many other street names that recall the old vocations of Florence, keeping the memory of these trades alive.

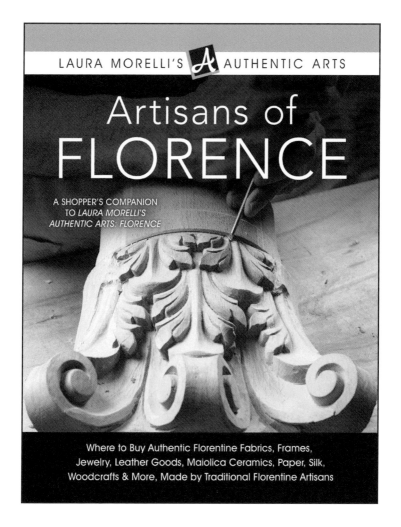

For up-to-date listings of Florentine artisans practicing traditional trades, download your free copy of **Artisans of Florence** by Laura Morelli from **www.LauraMorelli.com/Florence-ReaderGift**.

Index

126

About the Author

Laura Morelli earned a Ph.D. in art history from Yale University, where she was a Bass Writing Fellow and an Andrew W. Mellon Doctoral Fellow. She has taught college art history in the United States and Italy and has lived in five countries. She is the creator of the guidebook series that includes *Made in Italy*, *Made in France*, and *Made in the Southwest*, as well as an award-winning historical novel set in 16th-century Venice entitled *The Gondola Maker*. She is a frequent contributor to *National Geographic Traveler*, *USA Today*, and other national publications.

I hope you enjoyed this book! If you would like to join my email list to learn about events and new releases, sign up at www.lauramorelli.com.

—Laura Morelli

Also by Laura Morelli

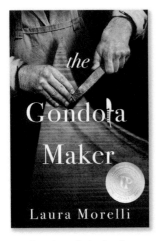

The Gondola Maker
Award-Winning Novel

**Made in Italy • Made in France
Made in the Southwest**

Laura Morelli's Authentic Arts Series:

**Florence • Naples & the Amalfi Coast • Paris
Provence & the French Riviera • Sardinia
Sicily • Tuscany & Umbria • Venice**

CPSIA information can be obtained
at www.ICGtesting.com
Printed in the USA
LVIC06n0211100415
434016LV00001B/1